DHARMA OCEAN SERIES

In a meeting with Samuel Bercholz, the president of Shambhala Publications, Ven. Chögyam Trungpa expressed his interest in publishing a series of 108 volumes, to be called the Dharma Ocean Series. "Dharma Ocean" is the translation of Chögyam Trungpa's Tibetan teaching name, Chökyi Gyatso. The Dharma Ocean Series consists primarily of edited transcripts of lectures and seminars given by Chögyam Trungpa during his seventeen years of teaching in North America. The goal of the series is to allow readers to encounter this rich array of teachings simply and directly rather than in an overly systematized or condensed form. At its completion, it will serve as the literary archive of the major works of this renowned Tibetan Buddhist teacher.

Series Editor: Judith L. Lief

D1289982

Books by Chögyam Trungpa

DHARMA OCEAN SERIES

Crazy Wisdom

Chögyam Trungpa

Edited by Sherab Chödzin

Shambhala • *Boston & London* • 2001

SHAMBHALA PUBLICATIONS, INC.
Horticultural Hall
300 Massachusetts Avenue
Boston, Massachusetts 02115
www.shambhala.com

9   8   7   6   5   4

Printed in the United States of America
♻ This edition is printed on acid-free paper that meets
the American National Standards Institute Z39.48 Standard.
♻ Shambhala makes every effort to print on recycled paper.
For more information please visit www.shambhala.com.
Distributed in the United States by Random House, Inc.,
and in Canada by Random House of Canada Ltd

LIBRARY OF CONGRESS CATALOGING-IN-PUBLICATION DATA
Trungpa, Chögyam, 1939–
Crazy wisdom / Chögyam Trungpa; edited by Sherab Chödzin
    p. cm.—(Dharma ocean series)   Includes index.
ISBN 978-0-87773-910-4   ISBN 978-1-57062-894-8 (pbk.)
    1. Padmasambhava, ca. 717–ca. 762.   2. Wisdom—
            Religious aspects—Buddhism.
    1. Chödzin, Sherab.   II. Title.   III. Series
            BQ7950.P327T75   1991
        294.3'4448—dc20   90-53378   CIP

Contents

Editor's Foreword

The Venerable Chögyam Trungpa Rinpoche gave two seminars on *crazy wisdom* in December 1972. Each lasted about a week. The first took place in an otherwise unoccupied resort hotel in the Tetons near Jackson Hole, Wyoming. The other happened in an old town hall cum gymnasium in the Vermont village of Barnet, just down the road from the meditation center founded by Trungpa Rinpoche now called Karme-Chöling, then known as Tail of the Tiger.

Rinpoche had arrived on this continent about two and a half years previous, in the spring of 1970. He had found an America bubbling with social change, animated by factors like hippyism, LSD, and the spiritual supermarket. In response to his ceaseless outpouring of teachings in a very direct, lucid, and down-to-earth style, a body of committed students had gathered, and more were arriving all the time. In the fall of 1972, he made his first tactical pause, taking a three-month retreat in a secluded house in the Massachusetts woods.

This was a visionary three months. Rinpoche seemed to contemplate the direction his work in America would take and the means at hand for its fulfillment. Important new plans were formulated. The last night of the retreat, he did not sleep. He told the few students present to use whatever was on hand and prepare a formal banquet. He himself spent hours in preparation for the banquet and did not appear until two in the morning—very beautifully groomed and dressed and buzzing with extraordinary energy. Conversation went on into the night. At one point, Rinpoche talked for two hours without stopping, giving an extremely vivid and detailed account of a dream he had had the night before. He left retreat with the dawn light and traveled all that day. That evening, still not having slept, he gave the first talk of the "Crazy Wisdom" seminar at Jackson Hole. It is possible that he went off that morning with a sense of beginning a new phase in his work. Certainly elements of such a new phase are described in the last talk of the seminar at Jackson Hole.

After the first Vajradhatu Seminary in 1973 (planned during the 1972 retreat) Trungpa Rinpoche's teaching style would change. His presentation would become much more methodical, geared toward guiding his students through the successive stages of the path. The "Crazy Wisdom" seminars thus belonged to the end of the introductory period of Rinpoche's teaching in North America, during which, by contrast, he showed a spectacular ability to convey all levels of the teachings at once. During this introductory phase there was a powerful fruitional atmosphere, bursting with the possibilities of the sudden path. Such an atmosphere prevailed as he made the basic teachings and advanced teachings into a single flow of profound instruction, while at the same time fiercely lopping away the omnipresent tentacles of spiritual materialism.

It might be helpful to look at these two seminars for a moment in the context of the battle against spiritual materialism. Though they had been planned in response to a request for teaching on the eight aspects of Padmasambhava, Trungpa Rinpoche had slightly shifted the emphasis and given the headline to crazy wisdom. His "experienced" students as well as the ones newly arriving had a relentless appetite for definite spiritual techniques or principles they could latch onto and identify with. The exotic iconography of the eight aspects of Padmasambhava, if presented too definitely, would have been bloody meat in the water for spiritually materialistic sharks. This may partly explain why a tidy hagiography of the eight aspects, with complete and consistent detail, was avoided, and the raw, ungarnished insight of crazy wisdom was delivered instead.

Some editing of this material from the original spoken presentation has been necessary for the sake of basic readability. However, nothing has been changed in the order of presentation, and nothing has been left out in the body of the talks. A great effort has been made not to cosmeticize Trungpa Rinpoche's language or alter his diction purely for the sake of achieving a conventionally presentable tone. Hopefully, the reader will enjoy those sentences of his that run between our mental raindrops and touch us where ordinary conceptual clarity could not. The reader will also hopefully appreciate that passages that remain dark on one reading may become luminously clear on another.

Here we have the mighty roaring of a great lion of dharma. May it put to flight the heretics and bandits of hope and fear. For the benefit of all beings, may his wishes continue to be fulfilled.

Crazy Wisdom Seminar I

JACKSON HOLE 1972

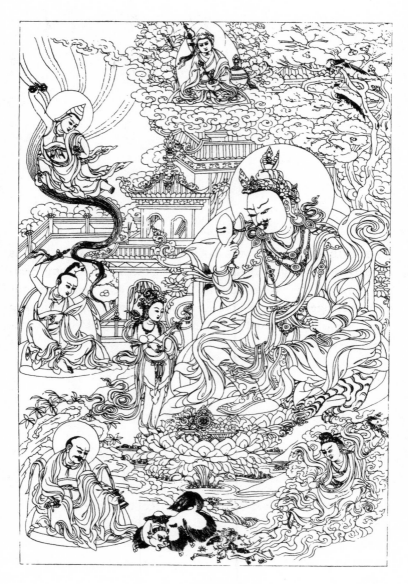

Pema Gyalpo

I

Padmasambhava and Spiritual Materialism

THE SUBJECT THAT WE ARE GOING TO DEAL WITH is an extraordinarily difficult one. It is possible that some people might get extraordinarily confused. Or people might very well get something out of it. We will be discussing Guru Rinpoche, or as he is often called in the West, Padmasambhava; we will be considering his nature and the various life-styles he developed in the process of working with students. This subject is very subtle, and some aspects of it are very difficult to put into words. I hope nobody will regard this humble attempt of mine as a definitive portrayal of Padmasambhava.

To begin with, we probably need some basic introduction to who Padmasambhava was; to how he fits into the context of the *buddhadharma* (the Buddhist teachings), in general; and to how he came to be so admired by Tibetans in particular.

Padmasambhava was an Indian teacher who brought the complete teachings of the buddhadharma to Tibet. He remains our source of inspiration even now, here in the West.

We have inherited his teachings, and from that point of view, I think we could say that Padmasambhava is alive and well.

I suppose the best way to characterize Padmasambhava for people with a Western or Christian cultural outlook is to say that he was a saint. We are going to discuss the depth of his wisdom and his life-style, his skillful way of relating with students. The students he had to deal with were Tibetans, who were extraordinarily savage and uncultured. He was invited to come to Tibet, but the Tibetans showed very little understanding of how to receive and welcome a great guru from another part of the world. They were very stubborn and very matter-of-fact—very earthy. They presented all kinds of obstacles to Padmasambhava's activity in Tibet. However, the obstacles did not come from the Tibetan people alone, but also from differences in climate, landscape, and the social situation as a whole. In some ways, Padmasambhava's situation was very similar to our situation here. Americans are hospitable, but on the other hand there is a very savage and rugged side to American culture. Spiritually, American culture is not conducive to just bringing out the brilliant light and expecting it to be accepted.

So there is an analogy here. In terms of that analogy, the Tibetans are the Americans and Padmasambhava is himself.

Before getting into details concerning Padmasambhava's life and teachings, I think it would be helpful to discuss the idea of a saint in the Buddhist tradition. The idea of a saint in the Christian tradition and the idea of a saint in the Buddhist tradition are somewhat conflicting. In the Christian tradition, a saint is generally considered someone who has direct communication with God, who perhaps is completely intoxicated with the Godhead and because of this is able to give out certain reassurances to people. People can look to the saint as an example of higher consciousness or higher development.

The Buddhist approach to spirituality is quite different. It is nontheistic. It does not have the principle of an external divinity. Thus there is no possibility of getting promises from the divinity and bringing them from there down to here. The Buddhist approach to spirituality is connected with awakening within oneself rather than with relating to something external. So the idea of a saint as someone who is able to expand himself to relate to an external principle, get something out of it, and then share that with others is difficult or nonexistent from the Buddhist point of view.

A saint in the Buddhist context—for example, Padmasambhava or a great being like the Buddha himself—is someone who provides an example of the fact that completely ordinary, confused human beings can wake themselves up; they can put themselves together and wake themselves up through an accident of life of one kind or another. The pain, the suffering of all kinds, the misery and the chaos that are part of life, begins to wake them, shake them. Having been shaken, they begin to question: "Who am I? What am I? How is it that all these things are happening?" Then they go further and realize that there is something in them that is asking these questions, something that is, in fact, intelligent and not exactly confused.

This happens in our own lives. We feel a sense of confusion—it seems to be confusion—but that confusion brings out something that is worth exploring. The questions that we ask in the midst of our confusion are potent questions, questions that we really have. We ask: "Who am I? What am I? What is this? What is life?" and so forth. Then we explore further and ask: "In fact, who on earth asked that question? Who is that person who asked the question 'Who am I?' Who is the person who asked, 'What is?' or even

'What is what is?' " We go on and on with this questioning, further and further inward. In some way, this is nontheistic spirituality in its fullest sense. External inspirations do not stimulate us to model ourselves on further external situations. Rather the external situations that exist speak to us of our confusion, and this makes us think more, think further. Once we have begun to do that, then of course there is the other problem: once we have found out who and what we are, how do we apply what we have learned to our living situation? How do we put it into practice?

There seem to be two possible approaches here. One is trying to live up to what we would *like* to be. The other is trying to live what we are. Trying to live up to what we would like to be is like pretending we are a divine being or a realized person, or whatever we might like to call the model. When we realize what is wrong with us, what our weakness is, what our problems and neuroses are, the automatic temptation is to try to act just the opposite, as though we have never heard of such a thing as our being wrong or confused. We tell ourselves: "Think positive! Act as though you're okay." Although we know that something is wrong with us on the level of the actual living situation, on the kitchen-sink level, we regard that as unimportant. "Let's forget those 'evil vibrations,' " we say. "Let's think the other way. Let's pretend to be good."

This approach is known in the Buddhist tradition as *spiritual materialism,* which means not being realistic, or to use hippie jargon, spacing out. "Let's forget the bad and pretend to be good." We could classify as spiritual materialism any approach—such as Buddhist, Hindu, Jewish, or Christian—that provides us with techniques to try to associate with the good, the better, the best—or the ultimately good, the divine.

When we begin associating ourselves with the good, it

makes us happy. We feel full of delight. We think, "At last I've found an answer!" That answer is that the only thing to do is regard ourselves as free already. Then, having established the position that we are free already, we just have to let all things flow.

Then we add a further touch to reinforce our spiritual materialism: everything that we do not know or did not understand in connection with our spiritual quest we connect with descriptions in various scriptures about that which is beyond mind, beyond words, ineffable—the ineffable Self, or whatever. We associate our own lack of understanding about what is going on with us with those unspoken, inexpressible things. This way our ignorance is made into the greatest discovery of all. We can connect this "great discovery" with a doctrinal supposition; for example, "the savior" or some interpretation of the scriptures.

Whereas before we didn't know anything at all, now we "know" something that we actually don't know. There *is* something ahead of us now. We cannot describe it in terms of words, concepts, and ideas, but we have discovered that, to begin with, it is a matter of twisting ourselves into the good. So we have this one thing to start with: we can directly and deliberately translate our confusion as being something that is not confused. We do this just because we are seeking pleasure, spiritual pleasure. In doing it, we affirm that the pleasure we are seeking is of an unknowable nature, because we actually have no idea what kind of spiritual pleasure we are going to get out of this maneuver. And all the spiritual interpretations of the scriptures referring to the unknowable can be applied to the fact that we do not know what we are trying to do spiritually. Nevertheless, we are definitely involved in spiritual conviction now, because we have suppressed our original doubts about who we are and what we are—our feeling that perhaps we might not be anything. We have suppressed that; we may not even know about it any more.

Having suppressed this embarrassment of ego that provided us with steppingstones to the unknown, the nature of which we did not understand, we end up with two games of confusion going on: a game of the unknown and a game of the transcendental unknown. Both of these are part of spiritual materialism. We do not know who or what we are, but we do know that we would like to be someone or something. We decide to go ahead with what we would like to be even though we do not know what that is. That is the first game. Then on top of that, in connection with being something, we would also like to know that there is something about the world or the cosmos that corresponds to this "something" that we are. We have a sense of finding this something that we want to know, but we actually can't understand it, so that becomes the transcendental unknown. Since we can't understand it, we say, "Let's make that bigger and more gigantic confusion into the spirituality of the infiniteness of the Godhead," or something like that.

This should give us some understanding of spiritual materialism. The danger of spiritual materialism is that under its influence we make all kinds of assumptions. First, there are the domestic or personal-level assumptions, which we make because we want to be happy. Second, there are the spiritual assumptions that are made because that transcendental, gigantic, greater discovery is left mysterious. This brings further great assumptions: we do not know what we are actually going to achieve by achieving that unknown thing, but nevertheless, we give it some vague description, such as "being absorbed into the cosmos." And since nobody has yet gone that far, if anybody questions this discovery of "absorption into the cosmos," then we just make up further logic or look for reinforcement from the scriptures or other authorities.

The result of all this is that we end up confirming our-selves and confirming that the experience we are proclaiming is a true experience. Nobody can question it. At some stage, there's no room left for questioning at all. Our whole out-look becomes completely established with no room left at all for questioning. This is what we could call achieving ego-hood, as opposed to achieving enlightenment. At that point, if I would like to practice my aggression and passion on you and you don't accept that, then that's your fault. You do not understand the ineffable spirituality, so you are at fault. The only way left for me to help you is to reduce you to a shrunken head, to take out your brain and heart. You be-come a mere puppet under my command.

That is a rough portrait of spiritual materialism. It is the first of the two possible approaches: trying to live up to what you would *like* to be. Now let's talk about the second possible approach, that of trying to live what you are.

This possibility is connected with seeing our confusion, or misery and pain, but not making those discoveries into an answer. Instead we explore further and further and further without looking for an answer. It is a process of working with ourselves, with our lives, with our psychology, without looking for an answer but seeing things as they are—seeing what goes on in our heads directly and simply, absolutely literally. If we can undertake a process like that, then there is a tremendous possibility that our confusion—the chaos and neurosis that goes on in our minds—might become a further basis for investigation. Then we look further and fur-ther and further. We don't make a big point or an answer out of any one thing. For example, we might think that be-cause we have discovered one particular thing that is wrong with us, that must be *it*, that must be the problem, that must be the answer. No. We don't fixate on that, we go further. "Why is that the case?" We look further and further. We ask: "Why is this so? Why is there spirituality? Why is there awakening? Why is there this moment of relief? Why is there such a thing as discovering the pleasure of spirituality? Why, why, why?" We go on deeper and deeper and deeper and deeper, until we reach the point where there is no answer. There is not even a question. Both question and answer die simultaneously at some point. They begin to rub each other too closely and they short-circuit each other in some way. At that point, we tend to give up hope of an answer, or of anything whatsoever, for that matter. We have no more hope, none whatsoever. We are purely hopeless. We could call this transcending hope, if you would like to put it in more genteel terms.

This hopelessness is the essence of crazy wisdom. It is hopeless, utterly hopeless. It is beyond hopelessness. (Of course it would be possible, if we tried to turn that hopelessness itself into some kind of solution, to become confused again, to say the least.)

The process is one of going further in and in and in without any reference point of spirituality, without any reference point of a savior, without any reference point of goodness or badness—without any reference points whatsoever! Finally we might reach the basic level of hopelessness, of transcending hope. This does not mean we end up as zombies. We still have all the energies; we have all the fascination of discovery, of seeing this process unfolding and unfolding and unfolding, going on and on. This process of discovery automatically recharges itself so that we keep going deeper and deeper and deeper. This process of going deeper and deeper is the process of crazy wisdom, and it is what characterizes a saint in the Buddhist tradition.

The eight aspects of Padmasambhava that we are going to discuss are connected with such a process of psychological penetration, of cutting through the surface of the psychological realm and then cutting through a further surface and infinitely further surfaces down through ever further depths of further surfaces, deeper and deeper. This is the process we involve ourselves in by discussing Padmasambhava's life, the eight aspects of Padmasambhava, and crazy wisdom.

In this context we see that the Buddhist approach to spirituality is one of ruthlessly cutting through any chance we might have of confirming ourselves at any particular stage of development on the spiritual path. When we discover that we have made some progress on the spiritual path, that discovery of progress is regarded as a hindrance to further progress. So we don't get a chance to rest, to relax, or to congratulate ourselves at all. It is a one-shot, ongoingly ruthless spiritual journey. And that is the essence of Padmasambhava's spirituality.

Padmasambhava had to work with the Tibetan people of those days. You can imagine it. A great Indian magician and pandit, a great *vidyadhara,* or tantric master, comes to the Land of Snow, Tibet. The Tibetans think he is going to teach them some beautiful spiritual teaching about how to know the essence of the mind. The expectations built up by the Tibetans are enormous. Padmasambhava's work is to cut through the Tibetans' layers and layers of expectations, through all their assumptions as to what spirituality might be. Finally, at the end of Padmasambhava's mission in Tibet, when he manifested as Dorje Trolö, all those layers of expectation were completely cut through. The Tibetans began to realize that spirituality is cutting through hope and fear as well as being the sudden discovery of intelligence that goes along with this process.

STUDENT: What is the difference between crazy wisdom and just being crazy? Some people might want to just go on being crazy and confused and excuse themselves by saying this is crazy wisdom. So what is the difference?

TRUNGPA RINPOCHE: Well, that is what I have been trying to explain through my whole talk, but let's try again. In the case of ordinary craziness, we are constantly trying to win the game. We might even try to turn craziness into a credential of some kind so we can come out ahead. We might try to magnetize people with passion or destroy them with aggression, or whatever. There's a constant game going on in the mind. Mind's game—constant strategies going on—might bring us a moment of relief occasionally, but that relief has to be maintained by further aggression. That kind of craziness has to maintain itself constantly, on and on.

In the case of the primordial craziness of crazy wisdom, we do not permit ourselves to get seduced by passion or aroused by aggression at all. We relate with these experiences as they are, and if anything comes up in the midst of that complete ordinariness and begins to make itself into a big deal, then we cut it down—without any special reference to what is good and what is bad. Crazy wisdom is just the action of truth. It cuts everything down. It does not even try to translate falseness into truthfulness, because that in itself is corruption. It is ruthless, because if you want the complete truth, if you want to be completely, wholly wholesome, then any suggestion that comes up of translating whatever arises into your terms, interpreting it in your terms, is not worth looking into. On the other hand, the usual crazy approach is completely up for that kind of thing—for making whatever comes up fit into your thing. You make it suit what you want to be, suit what you want to see. But crazy wisdom becomes completely accurate out of the moment of things as they are. This is the style of action of Padmasambhava.

STUDENT: How does discipline relate to being what you really are? I thought discipline meant imposing something on yourself.

TRUNGPA RINPOCHE: The most difficult discipline is to be what you are. Constantly trying to be what you are *not* is much easier, because we are trained to con either ourselves or others, to fit things into appropriate categories. Whereas if you take all of that away, the whole thing becomes too irritating, too boring. There's no room for talking yourself into anything. Everything is quite simple.

STUDENT: You often make use of your sense of humor in explaining things. Is sense of humor, the way you use it, the same as crazy wisdom?

TRUNGPA RINPOCHE: Not quite. Sense of humor is still too much slanted toward the other side, toward hope and fear. It's a dialectic mentality, whereas crazy wisdom is an overall approach.

STUDENT: Do we relate to hope and fear through the discipline of spiritual practice?

TRUNGPA RINPOCHE: That's a good point, actually. From this point of view, anything that is ruthless—anything that knows nothing of hope and fear—is related to spiritual practice.

Padmasambhava as a young bhikshu

The Trikaya

WE HAVE DISCUSSED TWO POSSIBLE APPROACHES to spirituality: spiritual materialism and transcending spiritual materialism. Padmasambhava's way is that of transcending spiritual materialism, of developing basic sanity. Developing basic sanity is a process of working on ourselves in which the path itself rather than the attainment of a goal becomes the working basis. The path itself is what constantly inspires us, rather than, in the style of the carrot and the donkey, promises about certain achievements that lie ahead of us. In other words, to make this perfectly clear, the difference between spiritual materialism and transcending spiritual materialism is that in spiritual materialism promises are used like a carrot held up in front of a donkey, luring him into all kinds of journeys; in transcending spiritual materialism, there is no goal. The goal exists in every moment of our life situation, in every moment of our spiritual journey.

In this way, the spiritual journey becomes as exciting and as beautiful as if we were buddha already. There are constant new discoveries, constant messages, and constant warnings. There is also constant cutting down, constant painful lessons—as well as pleasurable ones. The spiritual journey of transcending spiritual materialism is a complete journey rather than one that is dependent on an external goal.

It is this completeness of the journey that we are going to discuss in relation to Padmasambhava's life. This completeness can be described in terms of certain aspects: it contains basic space, or totality; it contains energy and play; and it also contains pragmatic application, or dealing with life situations as they are. We have three principles there: the totality as the whole sense of environment on the path, the sense of play on the path, and the sense of practicality on the path. These are the three categories that develop.

Before getting into the details of Padmasambhava's eight aspects, it would be good to discuss these three principles in terms of how Padmasambhava manifests them to us as path.

First, we have to look more closely at the nature of the path itself. The path is our effort, the energy that we put into the daily living situation; it consists of our trying to work with the daily living situation as a learning process—whether that situation is creative or destructive or whatever. If you spill a cup of coffee on your neighbor's table or if you just pass someone the salt, it's the same thing. These are the happenings that occur all the time in our life situations. We are constantly doing things, constantly relating with things or rejecting things. There is constant play. I am not particularly talking about spirituality at this point, but just daily existence: those events that happen all the time in our life situations. That is the path.

The path does not particularly have to be labeled as spiritual. It is just a simple journey, the journey that contains exchange with the reality of this and that—or with the unreality of it, if you prefer. Relating with these exchanges—the living process, the being process—is the path. We may be thinking of our path in terms of attaining enlightenment or of attaining egohood, or whatever. In any case, we never get stuck in any way at all. We might think we get stuck. We might feel bored with life and so forth; but we never really get bored or really get stuck. The repetitiousness of life is not really repetition. It is composed of constant happenings, situations constantly evolving, all the time. That is the path.

From this point of view, the path is neutral. It is not biased one way or the other. There is a constant journey happening, which began at the time of the basic split. We began to relate in terms of "the other," "me," "mine," "our," and so on. We began to relate with things as separate entities. The other is called "them" and this thing is called "I" or "me." The journey began right from there. That was the first creation of samsara and nirvana. Right at the beginning, when we decided to connect in some way with the energy of situations, we involved ourselves in a journey, in the path.

After that, we develop a certain way of relating with the path, and the path becomes conditioned toward either worldliness or spirituality. In other words, spirituality is not really the path, but spirituality is a way of conditioning our path, our energy.

Conditioning our path happens in terms of the three categories I have already mentioned. It happens, for example, in terms of the totality of experience, the first category. That is one aspect of *how* we relate to our path—in terms of the totality of our experience. The path is happening anyway, then we relate to it in a certain way, we take a certain attitude toward it. The path then becomes either a spiritual path or a mundane path. This is the way we relate to the path; this is how our motivation begins. And our motivation has the threefold pattern.

In the Buddhist tradition, these three aspects of the path are called *dharmakaya, sambhogakaya,* and *nirmanakaya.* The conditioning of the path happens in terms of those three aspects. The ongoing process of the path has a certain total attitude. The journey takes on a pattern that has an element of total basic sanity in it. This total sanity, or enlightened quality, is not particularly attractive in the ordinary sense. It is the sense of complete openness that we discussed earlier. It is this complete total openness that makes us able to transcend hope and fear. With this openness, we relate to things as they are rather than as we would like them to be. That basic sanity, that approach transcending hope and fear, is the attitude of enlightenment.

This attitude is very practical. It does not reject what comes up on the path, and it does not become attached to what comes up on the path. It just sees things as they are. So this is total, complete openness—complete willingness to look into whatever arises, to work with it, and to relate to it as part of the overall process. This is the dharmakaya mentality of all-encompassing space, of including everything without bias. It is a larger way of thinking, a greater way of viewing things, as opposed to being petty, finicky.

We are taking the dharmakaya approach as long as we do not relate to the world as our enemy. The world is our opportune situation; it is what we have to work with. Nothing that arises makes us have to fight with the world. The world is the extraordinarily rich situation that is there; it is full of resources for us. This basic approach of generosity and richness is the dharmakaya's approach. It is total positive thinking. This greater vision is the first attitude in relation to the path.

Then we have the second attitude, connected with the sambhogakaya. Things are open and spacious and workable as we have said, but there is something more. We also need to relate to the sparkiness, the energy, the flashes and aliveness that take place within that openness. That energy, which includes aggression, passion, ignorance, pride, jealousy, and so forth, also has to be acknowledged. Anything that goes on in the realm of the mind can be accepted as the glittering light that shines through the massiveness of the spiritual path. It shines constantly, surprises us constantly. There is another corner of our being that is so alive, so energetic and powerful. There are discoveries happening all the time. That is the sambhogakaya's way of relating with the path.

Thus the path contains the larger sense of total acceptance of things as they are; and the path also contains what we might call fascination with the exciting discoveries within situations. It is worth repeating here that we are not putting our experiences into pigeonholes of virtuous or religious or worldly. We are just relating with the things that happen in our life situations. Those energies and passions that we encounter on our journey present us with continual discoveries of different facets of ourselves, different profiles of ourselves. At that point, things become rather interesting. After all, we are not so blank or flat as we imagined ourselves to be.

Then we have the third kind of relationship with the path, which is connected with the nirmanakaya. This is the basic practicality of existing in the world. We have the totality, we have the various energies, and then we have how to function in the world as it is, the living world. This last aspect demands tremendous awareness and effort. We cannot simply leave it to the totality and the energy to take care of everything; we have to put some discipline into our approach to our life situations. All the disciplines and techniques spoken of in spiritual traditions are connected with this nirmanakaya principle of application on the path. There is practicing meditation, working with the intellect, taking a further interest in relationships with each other, developing fundamental compassion and a sense of communication, and developing knowledge or wisdom that is capable of looking at a whole situation and seeing the ways in which things might be workable. All those are nirmanakaya disciplines.

Taken together, the three principles, or three stages—dharmakaya, sambhogakaya, nirmanakaya—provide us with a complete basis for our spiritual journey. Because of them, the journey and our attitude toward it become something workable, something we can deal with directly and intelligently, without having to relegate it to some vague category like "the mysteriousness of life."

In terms of our psychological state, these principles each have another characteristic, which it is worth mentioning here. As a psychological state, the dharmakaya is basic being. It is a totality in which confusion and ignorance have never existed; it is total existence that *never needs any reference point*. The sambhogakaya is that which continually contains spontaneous energy, because it *never depends on any cause-and-effect kind of energy*. The nirmanakaya is self-existing fulfillment in relation to which *no strategizing about how to function is necessary*. Those are the psychological aspects of buddhanature that develop.

In looking at Padmasambhava's life and his eight aspects, we will find those three principles. Seeing those psychological principles in action in Padmasambhava's life can help us to not regard Padmasambhava purely as some mythical figure that no one has ever met. Those are principles that we can work on together, and each one of you can work on them in relation to yourself.

STUDENT: Are the eight aspects of Padmasambhava like eight stages that we can work through in trying to make a breakthrough in our own psychological development?

TRUNGPA RINPOCHE: Actually, the eight aspects are not

really lineal, successive levels of development. What we have is more a single situation with eight aspects—a central principle surrounded by eight types of manifestation. There are eight aspects of all kinds of situations.

Psychologically, we could make some kind of breakthrough by relating with that. You see, as it tells us in the scriptures, when Padmasambhava manifested as the eight aspects, he was already enlightened. The eight aspects were not his spiritual journey, but he was expressing himself, dancing with situations. He was already coming out with his crazy-wisdom expressions.

What I'm trying to say is, we could find all those eight aspects within ourselves, in one working situation. We could connect with them. We could break through with all eight simultaneously.

S: So it's definitely not a linear progression like the ten *bhumis*.

TR: You see, here we are talking about the sudden path, the direct or sudden path of tantra. This is realization that does not depend on a progressive, external build-up or unmasking. It is realization eating out from the inside rather than unmasking taking place from the outside. Eating out from the inside is the tantric approach. In some sense, this supersedes the ten bhumis, or stages, of the bodhisattva path. We are discussing more the vajralike samadhi of the Buddha and his way of relating with things, which of course is connected with buddha-nature; we are approaching that here as a sudden, direct transmission, a direct way, without going through the paramitas or the bhumis. The approach here is to regard oneself as being a buddha already. Buddha is the path rather than the goal. We are working from the inside outward. The mask is falling off by itself.

STUDENT: Was Padmasambhava already buddha when he was born?

TRUNGPA RINPOCHE: He was more an awake person than a fully realized buddha. He was the dharmakaya principle trying to manifest itself on the sambhogakaya level and then beginning to relate to the world outside. Thus he could be regarded as a person who was a potential buddha at birth and who then broke the barriers to the fulfillment of that potential ruthlessly and without fear. He attained instantaneous enlightenment on one spot, and it seems that we could do the same.

STUDENT: Is this connected with the idea of our having to take a leap that you have spoken about so often?

TRUNGPA RINPOCHE: This has more to do with the *attitude* of taking a leap than actually taking the leap. You are willing to leap, so then there is the situation of leaping. The important thing here is the basic spirit or outlook you have, rather than just the particular application of how you handle things. It is something much bigger than that.

STUDENT: You've talked a lot about ruthlessness and fearlessness. What are you ruthless toward? Do you just ruthlessly assume a particular psychological attitude?

TRUNGPA RINPOCHE: The whole point of ruthlessness is that when you are ruthless, no one can con you. No one can seduce you in an unhealthy direction. It is ruthlessness in that sense rather than in the conventional sense of illogical aggression—such as in the case of Mussolini or Hitler or someone like that. You cannot be conned or seduced; you would not accept that. Even attempts to seduce you arouse energy that is destructive toward that attempted seduction. If you are completely open and completely aroused in terms of crazy wisdom, no one can lure you into their territory.

S: You can maintain the ruthlessness—

TR: You don't maintain the ruthlessness. Your ruthlessness

is maintained by others. You don't maintain anything at all. You just *be* there, and whatever situation comes to you, you just project back. Take the example of fire. It does not possess its destructiveness. That just happens. When you put something in the fire or try to kill the fire, its offensive power just comes out. It is the organic or chemical nature of fire.

S: When these things come at you, then you have to be ruthless in order to repel them, right? Then it seems that a judgment has to be made as to right and wrong, as to whether what is coming at you is positive or negative, and whether to be compassionate or ruthless.

TR: I don't think so. That's the whole point of the transcendental type of ruthlessness. It does not need judgment. The situation brings the action. You simply react, because the elements contain aggression. If the elements are interfered with or dealt with in an irreverent or unskillful way, they hit you back.

Ruthlessness may seem to survive on a sense of relativity, of "this" versus "that," but in fact it actually does not. It is absolute. The others present a relative notion, which you cut through. This state of being is not on a relative level at all. In other words, this absoluteness cuts through the relative notion that comes to it, but still it remains self-contained.

S: That would make it very isolated, very lonely.

TR: No, I don't think so, because absolute means *everything*. So you have more than you need, so to speak.

S: Are you saying that hopelessness and fearlessness are the same thing?

TR: Yes. They are the ultimate thing, if you are able to work with that. They are the ultimate thing.

STUDENT: How does ruthlessness apply to the destruction of ego? Ruthlessness seems so uncompassionate, almost ego-like itself.

TRUNGPA RINPOCHE: Well, it is ego's intensity that brings forth "uncompassionate" measures. In other words, when neurosis and confusion reach an extreme point, the only way to correct the confusion is by destroying it. You have to completely shatter the whole thing. That process of destruction is demanded by the confusion itself rather than it being a question of somebody thinking it is a good idea to destroy the confusion by force. No other thinking is involved. The intensity of confusion itself demands its own destruction. Ruthlessness is just putting that energy into action. It is just letting that energy burn itself out rather than your killing something. You just let ego's neurosis commit suicide rather than killing it. That's the ruthlessness. Ego is killing itself ruthlessly, and you are providing the accommodation for that.

This is not warfare. You are there, and therefore it happens. On the other hand, if you are not there, there is the possibility of scapegoats and sidetracks of all kinds. But if you are there, you don't even actually have to be ruthless. Just be there; from the point of view of ego, that is ruthless.

3

Primordial Innocence

THE DISCOVERY OF THE PATH and the appropriate attitude toward it have a certain function spiritually. The path can make it possible to connect with basic, primordial, innocent being.

We put so much emphasis on pain and confusion that we forget basic innocence. The usual approach that we take toward spirituality is to look for some experience that might enable us to rediscover our adulthood rather than go back to our innocent childlike quality. We have been fooled into looking for a way to become completely grown-up and respectable, as it were, or psychologically sound.

This seems to correspond to the basic idea we have of enlightenment. An enlightened person is supposed to be more or less an old-wise-man type: not quite like an old professor, but perhaps an old father who can supply sound advice on how to handle all of life's problems or an old grandmother who knows all the recipes and all the cures. That seems to be the current fantasy that exists in our culture concerning enlightened beings. They are old and wise, grown-up and solid.

Tantra has a different notion of enlightenment, which is

connected with youth and innocence. We can see this pattern in Padmasambhava's life story, where the awakened state of mind is portrayed not as old and adult but as young and free. Youth and freedom in this case are connected with the birth of the awakened state of mind. The awakened state of mind has the quality of morning, of dawn—fresh and sparkling, completely awake. This is the quality of the birth of Padmasambhava.

Having identified ourselves with the path and the proper attitude toward the path, we suddenly discover that there is something beautiful about it. The path has a freshness to it that contrasts sharply with the monotony of going through a program of various practices. New discoveries are being made. New discovery is the birth of Padmasambhava.

Padmasambhava was born in a lotus flower on a lake in Uddiyana. He had the appearance of an eight-year-old. He was inquisitive, bright, youthful, untouched by anything. Since he had never been touched by anything, he was not afraid to touch anything. He was surrounded by dakinis making offerings to him and playing music. There were even beasts, wild animals, all around paying homage to him on this fresh, unpolluted lake—Lake Dhanakosha in Uddiyana, somewhere in the Himalayan region of Afghanistan. The landscape was similar to that of Kashmir, with very fresh mountain air and snow-capped mountains all around. There was a sense of freshness and at the same time some sense of wildness.

For an infant to be born in such a wild, desolate place in the middle of a lake on a lotus is beyond the grasp of conceptual mind. For one thing, a child cannot be born from a lotus. For another, such a wild mountain region is too hostile to accommodate the birth of a child, and a healthy one at that. Such a birth is impossible. But then, impossible things happen, things beyond our imagination. In fact, impossible things happen before our imagination even occurs, so we could appropriately describe them as unimaginable— even "out of sight" or "far out."

Padmasambhava was born in a lotus on this lake. He was born a prince, young and cute, but also bright, terrifyingly bright. His bright eyes look at you. He is not afraid to touch anything at all. Sometimes it is embarrassing to be around him, this good and beautiful eight-year-old infant.

The awakened state of mind could as well be infantlike as grown-up, the way we usually imagine grown-up. Life batters us, confuses us, but somebody manages to cross the turbulent river of life and find the answer; somebody works very, very hard and finally achieves peace of mind. That is our usual idea, but that is not how it is with Padmasambhava. He is inexperienced. Life has not battered him at all. He was just born out of a lotus in the middle of a lake in Afghanistan somewhere. That is a very exciting message, extraordinarily exciting. One can be enlightened and be infantlike. That is in accord with things as they are: if we are awake, we are only an infant. At the first stage of our experience, we are just an infant. We are innocent, because we have gone back to our original state of being.

Padmasambhava was invited to the court of King Indrabhuti. The king had asked his gardeners to collect fresh flowers—lotuses and mountain flowers—in the region of the lake. To one of the gardeners' surprise, he discovered a gigantic lotus with a child sitting on it—very happily. He did not want to touch the child; he was afraid of the mysteriousness of it. He reported back to the king, who told him to bring the child as well as the flower. Padmasambhava was enthroned and crowned as the Prince of Uddiyana. He was called Padma Raja, or Pema Gyalpo in Tibetan, "the Lotus King."

It is possible for us to discover our own innocence and

childlike beauty, the princelike quality in us. Having discovered all our confusions and neuroses, we begin to realize that they are harmless or helpless. Then gradually we find the innocent-child quality in us. Of course, this is quite different from the primal-scream type of idea. And it does not mean that we are being *reduced* to a child. Rather, we discover the child*like* quality in us. We become fresh, inquisitive, sparkling; we want to know more about the world, more about life. All of our preconceptions have been stripped away. We begin to realize ourselves—it is like a second birth. We discover our innocence, our primordial quality, our eternal youth.

The first breakthrough presents us with our childlike quality, but we are still somewhat apprehensive about how to deal with life, though we are not terrified by it. There is a sense of reaching out our hand and beginning to explore all the unknown areas for the first time. Our experience of duality, what we thought we knew, our preconceptions—all that has become false, has fallen apart. Now, for the first time, we recognize the real quality of the path. We give up our ego reservations, or at least realize them.

The more we realize ego and ego's neurosis, the closer we are to that infantlike state of mind of not knowing how to handle the next step in life. Often people ask: "Suppose I do meditate, then what am I going to do? If I attain a peaceful state of mind, how am I going to deal with my enemies and my superiors?" We actually ask very infantlike questions. "If thus-and-such happens as we progress along the path, then what's going to happen next?" It is very childlike, infantlike; it is a fresh discovery of perception, a new discovery of a sense of things as they are.

So Padmasambhava lived in the palace; he was taken care of and entertained. At a certain point he was asked to marry. Because of his innocence, he had great reservations about this, but he finally decided to go ahead. The young prince grew up. He explored sexuality and the marriage system and related with a wife. Gradually he came to realize that the world around him was not all that delicate any more, not as delicate as lotus petals. The world was exciting, playful. It was like being given, for the first time, a substantial toy that could be bashed about, unscrewed, taken apart, put back together again.

This is a very moving story of a journey ever further outward. Starting from the basic innocence of the dharmakaya level, which is the embryonic state of buddha-nature, we have to come out, step out. We have to relate with the playfulness of the world as it is on the sambhogakaya and nirmanakaya levels.

Padmasambhava as a baby represents that complete, childlike state in which there is no duality; there is no "this" and no "that." This state is completely all-pervading. There is also a sense of freshness, because this state is total, it is all over, there is no reference point. If there is no reference point, then there is nothing to pollute one's concepts or ideas. It is one absolute ultimate thing altogether.

Starting from that, Padmasambhava, having married, became more playful. He even began to experiment with his aggression, finding that he could use his strength to throw things and things could get broken. And he carried this to an extreme, knowing that he had the potential for crazy wisdom within him. He danced holding two scepters—a *vajra* and a *trident*—on the palace roof. He dropped his vajra and trident, and they fell and hit a mother and her son who were walking below, simultaneously killing them both. They happened to be the wife and son of one of the king's ministers. The vajra hit the child's head, and the trident struck the mother's heart.

Very playful! (I am afraid this is not quite a respectable story.)

This event had serious repercussions. The ministers decided to exert their influence on the king and asked him to send Padmasambhava away, to exile him from the kingdom. Padmasambhava's crime was committed in the wildness of exploring things, which is still on the sambhogakaya level— in the realm of experiencing things and their subtleties, and of exploring birth and death as well. So the king exiled Padmasambhava. This was much to the king's own regret, but the play of the phenomenal world had to be legal. The phenomenal world is a very basic legal setup. The play of phenomena has cause and effect constantly happening within it.

This does not mean to say that Padmasambhava was subject to karma. Rather, he was exploring the legality of karma—karmic interplays with the outside world, the confused world. It was that confused world that molded him to be a teacher, rather than his proclaiming himself, saying, "I am a teacher" or "I am the savior of the world." He never claimed anything like that. But the world began to mold Padmasambhava into the shape of a teacher or savior. And one of the expressions of the world's doing that, which made this process able to proceed, was the fact that he performed this violent action and therefore had to be expelled from King Indrabhuti's kingdom and had to go to the charnel ground of Silwa Tsal ("Cool Grove"), supposedly somewhere in the region of Bodhgaya in southern India.

This infant quality and the exploratory quality that develops in our being as we begin to work on the spiritual path require working with dangers as well as working with pleasures of all kinds. That childlike quality automatically tends toward the world outside, having already realized that the sudden, instant enlightened state of mind is not the end but the beginning of the journey. The sudden awakeness happens, and then we become an infant. Then after that, we explore how to work with phenomena, how to dance with phenomena, and at the same time, how to relate with confused people. Working with confused people automatically draws us into certain shapes according to the teachings the confused people require and the situations that are required in order to relate with them.

STUDENT: Could you say a bit more about the dharmakaya principle and the idea of totality as well as a bit more about the sambhogakaya and nirmanakaya?

TRUNGPA RINPOCHE: It seems that the dharmakaya principle is that which accommodates everything. It accommodates any extremes, whether the extremes are there or not—it doesn't really make any difference. It is the totality in which there is tremendous room to move about. The sambhogakaya principle is the energy that is involved with that totality and that puts further emphasis on that totality. The totality aspect of the dharmakaya is like the ocean, and the sambhogakaya aspect is like the waves of that ocean, which make the statement that that ocean does exist. The nirmanakaya aspect is like a ship on the ocean, which makes the whole situation into a pragmatic and workable one—you can sail across the ocean.

S: How does this relate to confusion?

TR: Confusion is the other partner. If there is understanding, that understanding usually has its own built-in limitation of understanding. Thus confusion is there automatically until the absolute level is reached, where understanding does not need its own help, because the entire situation is an understood situation.

STUDENT: How does this apply to daily life?

TRUNGPA RINPOCHE: Well, in daily life, it's just the

same. Working with the totality, there is basic room to work with life, and also there is energy and practicality involved. In other words, we are not limited to a particular thing. A lot of the frustration we have with our lives comes from the feeling that there are inadequate means to change and improvise with our life situations. But those three principles of dharmakaya, sambhogakaya, and nirmanakaya provide us with tremendous possibilities for improvisation. There are endless resources of all kinds we could work with.

STUDENT: What was Padmasambhava's relationship with King Indrabhuti all about? How did it relate to his development from his basic innocence?

TRUNGPA RINPOCHE: King Indrabhuti was his first audience, the first representative of samsara. Indrabhuti's bringing him to the palace was the starting point for learning how to work with students, confused people. Indrabhuti provided a strong father-figure representation of confused mind.

STUDENT: Who were the mother and son who were killed?

TRUNGPA RINPOCHE: There have been several interpretations of that in the scriptures and commentaries concerning Padmasambhava's life. Since the vajra is connected with skillful means, the child killed by the vajra is the opposite of skillful means, which is aggression. The trident is connected with wisdom, so the mother killed by it represents ignorance. And there are also further justifications based on the karma of previous lives: the son was so-and-so and committed thus-and-such a bad karmic act, and the same with the mother. But I don't think we have to go into those details. It gets a bit too complicated. The story of Padmasambhava at this point is in a completely different dimension—

that of the psychological world. It comes down to a practical level, so to speak, when he gets to Tibet and begins dealing with the Tibetans. Before that, it is very much in the realm of mind.

STUDENT: Is there any analogy between these two deaths and the sword of Manjushri cutting the root of ignorance? Or the Buddha's speaking about *shunyata,* emptiness, and some of his disciples having heart attacks?

TRUNGPA RINPOCHE: I don't think so. The sword of Manjushri is very much oriented toward practice on the path, but the story of Padmasambhava is related with the goal. Once you have already experienced the sudden flash of enlightenment, how do you handle yourself beyond that? The Manjushri story and the story of the *Heart Sutra* and all the other stories of sutra teaching correspond to the hinayana and mahayana levels and are designed for the seeker on the path. What we are discussing here is the umbrella notion— the notion of coming down from the top: having already attained enlightenment, how do we work with further programs? The story of Padmasambhava is a manual for buddhas—and each of us is one of them.

STUDENT: Was he experimenting with motive?

TRUNGPA RINPOCHE: Well, in the realm of the dharmakaya, it is very difficult to say what is and what is not the motive. There isn't anything at all.

STUDENT: I would like to know more about the contrasting metaphors of eating out from the inside and stripping away layers from the outside. If I understood correctly, stripping away is the bodhisattva path, whereas on the tantric path, you're eating out from the inside. But I really don't understand the metaphors.

TRUNGPA RINPOCHE: The whole point is that tantra is contagious. It involves a very powerful substance, which is buddha-nature eating out from the inside rather than being reached by stripping away layers from the outside. In Padmasambhava's life story, we are discussing the goal as the path, rather than the path as the path. It is a different perspective altogether; it is not the point of view of sentient beings trying to attain enlightenment, but the point of view of an enlightened person trying to relate with sentient beings. That is why the tantric approach is that of eating outward, from the inside to the outside. Padmasambhava's difficulties with his father, King Indrabhuti, and with the murder of the child and his mother are all connected with sentient beings. We are telling the story from the inside rather than looking at somebody else's newsreel taken from the outside.

STUDENT: How does the eating away outward take place?

TRUNGPA RINPOCHE: Through dealing with situations skillfully. The situations are already created for you, and you just go out and launch yourself along with them. It is a self-existing jigsaw puzzle that has been put together by itself.

STUDENT: Is it the dharmakaya aspect that diffuses hope and fear?

TRUNGPA RINPOCHE: Yes, that seems to be the basic thing. Hope and fear are all-pervading, like a haunted situation. But the dharmakaya takes away the haunt altogether.

STUDENT: Are you saying that the story of Padmasambhava, from his birth in the lotus through his destroying all the layers of students' expectations and finally manifesting as Dorje Trolö, is moving from the dharmakaya slowly into the nirmanakaya?

TRUNGPA RINPOCHE: Yes, that is what I have been trying to get at. So far he has risen out of the dharmakaya and has just gotten to the fringe of the sambhogakaya. Sambhogakaya is the energy principle, or the dance principle—dharmakaya being the total background.

S: Is it that hope and fear have to fade away before the——

TR: Before the dance can take place. Yes, definitely.

STUDENT: Is the sambhogakaya energy the energy that desire and anger are attached to?

TRUNGPA RINPOCHE: The sambhogakaya level doesn't seem to be that. It is the positive aspect that is left by the unmasking process. In other words, you get the absence of aggression and that absence is turned into energy.

S: So when the defilements are transformed into wisdom——

TR: Transmuted. It is even more than transmutation—I don't know what sort of a word there is. The defilements are being so completely related to that their function becomes useless but their nonfunctioning becomes useful. There is another kind of energy in sambhogakaya.

STUDENT: There seems to be some kind of cosmic joke about the whole thing. What you're saying is that you have to take the first step, but you can't take the first step until you take the first step.

TRUNGPA RINPOCHE: Yes, you have to be pushed into it. That is where the relationship between teacher and student comes in. Somebody has to push. That is the very primitive level at the beginning.

S: Are you pushing?

TR: I think so.

Vajradhara

4

Eternity and the Charnel Ground

I WOULD LIKE TO MAKE SURE that what we have already discussed is quite clear. The birth of Padmasambhava is like a sudden experience of the awakened state. The birth of Padmasambhava cannot take place unless there is an experience of the awakened state of mind that shows us our innocence, our infantlike quality. And Padmasambhava's experiences with King Indrabhuti of Uddiyana are connected with going further after one has already had a sudden glimpse of awake. That seems to be the teaching, or message, of Padmasambhava's life so far.

Now let us go on to the next aspect of Padmasambhava. Having experienced the awakened state of mind, and having had experiences of sexuality and aggression and all the pleasures that exist in the world, there is still uncertainty about how to work with those worldly processes. Padmasambhava is not uncertain in the sense of being confused, but about how to teach, how to connect with the audience. The students themselves are apprehensive, because for one thing they have never dealt with an enlightened person before. Working with an enlightened person is extraordinarily sensitive and pleasurable, but at the same time, it could be quite destructive. If we did the wrong thing, we might be hit or destroyed. It is like playing with fire.

So Padmasambhava's experience of relating with samsaric mind continues. He is expelled from the palace, and he goes on making further discoveries. The discovery that he makes at this point is eternity. Eternity here is the sense that the experience of awake is constantly going on without any fluctuations—and without any decisions to be made, for that matter. At this point, in connection with the second aspect, the decisionlessness of Padmasambhava's experience of dealing with sentient beings becomes prominent.

Padmasambhava's second aspect is called Vajradhara. Vajradhara is a principle or a state of mind that possesses fearlessness. The fear of death, the fear of pain and misery— all such fears—have been transcended. Having transcended those states, the eternity of life goes on beyond them. Such eternity is not particularly dependent on life situations and whether or not we make them healthier or whether or not we achieve longevity. It is not dependent on anything of that nature.

We are discussing a sense of eternity that could apply to our own lives as well. This attitude of eternity is quite different from the conventional spiritual idea of eternity. The conventional idea is that if you attain a certain level of spiritual one-upmanship, you will be free from birth and death. You will exist forever and be able to watch the play of the world and have power over everything. It is the notion of the superman who cannot be destroyed, the good savior who helps everybody using his Superman outfit. This general notion of eternity and spirituality is somewhat distorted, somewhat cartoonlike: The spiritual superman has power over others, and therefore he can attain longevity, which is a continuity of his power over others. Of course he does also help others at the same time.

As Vajradhara, Padmasambhava's experience of eternity—
or his existence as eternity—is quite different. There is a
sense of continuity, because he has transcended the fear of
birth, death, illness, and any kind of pain. There is a constant living, electric experience that he is not really living
and existing, but rather it is the world that lives and exists,
and therefore he is the world and the world is him. He has
power over the world because he does not have power over
the world. He does not want to hold any kind of position as
a powerful person at this point.

Vajradhara is a Sanskrit name. *Vajra* means "indestructible," *dhara* means "holder." So it is as the "holder of indestructibility" or "holder of immovability" that Padmasambhava attains the state of eternity. He attains it because he
was born as an absolutely pure and completely innocent
child—so pure and innocent that he had no fear of exploring
the world of birth and death, of passion and aggression.
That was the preparation for his existence, but his exploration continued beyond that level. Birth and death and other
kinds of threats might be seen by samsaric or confused mind
as solid parts of a solid world. But instead of seeing the
world as a threatening situation, he began to see it as his
home. In this way he attained the primordial state of eternity, which is quite different from the state of perpetuating
ego. Ego needs to maintain itself constantly; it constantly
needs further reassurance. But in this case, through transcending spiritual materialism, Padmasambhava attained an
ongoing, constant state based on being inspired by fellow
confused people, sentient beings.

The young prince, recently turned out of his palace,
roamed around the charnel ground. There were floating skeletons with floating hair. Jackals and vultures, hovering
about, made their noises. The smell of rotten bodies was all
over the place. The genteel young prince seemed to fit in to

that scene quite well, as incongruous as it might seem. He was quite fearless, and his fearlessness became accommodation as he roamed through the jungle charnel ground of Silwa Tsal near Bodhgaya. There were awesome-looking trees and terrifying rock shapes and the ruins of a temple. The whole feeling was one of death and desolation. He'd been abandoned, he'd been kicked out of his kingdom, but still he roamed and played about as if nothing had happened. In fact, he regarded this place as another palace in spite of all its terrifying sights. Seeing the impermanence of life, he discovered the eternity of life, the constant changing process of death and birth taking place all the time.

There was a famine in the vicinity. People were continually dying. Sometimes half-dead bodies were brought to the charnel ground, because people were so exhausted with the constant play of death and sickness. There were flies, worms, maggots, and snakes. Padmasambhava, this young prince who had recently been turned out of a jewel-laden palace, made a home out of this; seeing no difference at all between this charnel ground and a palace, he took delight in it.

Our civilized world is so orderly that we do not see places like this charnel ground. Bodies are kept in their coffins and buried quite respectably. Nevertheless there are the greater charnel grounds of birth, death, and chaos going on around us all the time. We encounter these charnel-ground situations in our lives constantly. We are surrounded by half-dead people, skeletons everywhere. But still, if we identify with Padmasambhava, we could relate with that fearlessly. We could be inspired by this chaos—so much so that chaos could become order in some sense. It could become orderly chaos rather than just confused chaos, because we would be able to relate with the world as it is.

Padmasambhava went and found the nearest cave, and he meditated on the principle of the eternity of buddha-nature:

buddha-nature is eternally existing, without being threatened by anything at all. Realization of that principle is one of the five stages of a vidyadhara. It is the first stage, called the vidyadhara of eternity.

Vidyadhara means "he who holds the scientific knowledge" or "he who has achieved complete crazy wisdom." So the first stage of crazy wisdom is the wisdom of eternity. Nothing threatens us at all; everything is an ornament. The greater the chaos, the more everything becomes an ornament. That is the state of Vajradhara.

We might ask how a young, innocent prince came to have such training that he was able to handle those charnel-ground situations. We might ask such a question, because we generally assume that in order to handle something we need training: we have to have benefited from an educational system. We have to have read books on how to live in a charnel ground and been instructed on what is appropriate and what is not appropriate to eat there. No training was necessary for Padmasambhava, because he was enlightened at the moment of his birth. He was coming out of the dharmakaya into the sambhogakaya, and a sudden flash of enlightenment does not need training. It does not require an educational system. It is inborn nature, not dependent on any kind of training at all.

In fact the whole concept of needing training for things is a very weak approach, because it makes us feel we cannot possess the potential in us, and that therefore we have to make ourselves better than we are, we have to try to compete with heroes or masters. So we try to imitate those heroes and masters, believing that finally, by some process of psychophysical switch, we might be able to become *them*. Although we are not actually them, we believe we could become them purely by imitating—by pretending, by deceiving ourselves constantly that we are what we are not. But when this sudden flash of enlightenment occurs, such hypocrisy doesn't exist. You do not have to pretend to be something. You *are* something. You have certain tendencies existing in you in any case. It is just a question of putting them into practice.

Still, Padmasambhava's discovery might feel somewhat desolate and slightly terrifying from our point of view if we imagine him meditating in a cave, surrounded by corpses and terrifying animals. But somehow we do have to relate with that in our personal life situations. We cannot con the existing experience of life; we cannot con our experiences or change them by having some unrealistic belief that things are going to be okay, that in the end everything is going to be beautiful. If we take that approach, then things are not going to be okay. For the very reason that we expect things to be good and beautiful, they won't be.

When we have such expectations, we are approaching things entirely from the wrong angle. Beauty is competing with ugliness, and pleasure is competing with pain. In this realm of comparison, nothing is going to be achieved at all.

We might say: "I've been practicing; I've been seeking enlightenment, nirvana, but I've been constantly pushed back. At the beginning I got some kind of kick out of those practices. I thought I was getting somewhere. I felt beautiful, blissful, and I thought I could get even better, get beyond even that. But then nothing happened. Practice became monotonous, and then I began to look for another solution, something else. Then at the same time I thought: 'I'm starting to be unfaithful to the practices I've been given. I shouldn't be looking for other practices. I shouldn't look elsewhere, I should have faith, I should stick with it. Okay, let's do it.' So I stick with it. But it is still uncomfortable, monotonous. In fact, it is irritating, too painful."

We go on and on this way. We repeat ourselves. We build something up and make ourselves believe in it. We say to

ourselves: "Now I should have faith. If I have faith, if I believe, I'm going to be saved." We try to prefabricate faith in
some way and get a momentary kick out of it. But then it
ends up the same way again and again and again—we don't
get anything out of it. There are always those problems with
that approach to spirituality.

In Padmasambhava's approach to spirituality, we are not
looking for a kick, for inspiration, or bliss. Instead, we are
digging into life's irritations, diving into the irritations and
making a home out of that. If we are able to make a home
out of those irritations, then the irritations become a source
of great joy, transcendental joy, *mahasukha*—because there is
no pain involved at all. This kind of joy is no longer related
with pain or contrasted with pain at all. So the whole thing
becomes precise and sharp and understandable, and we are
able to relate with it.

Padmasambhava's further adaptation to the world through
the attitude of eternity, the first of the five stages of a vidyadhara, plays an important part in the study of the rest of
Padmasambhava's aspects. This subject comes up again and
again.

STUDENT: Why couldn't Padmasambhava's making his
home in the charnel ground be considered masochism?

TRUNGPA RINPOCHE: To begin with, there is no sense of
aggression at all. He is not out to win anybody over. He is
just there, relating to things as they are. In masochism, you
have to have someone to blame, someone to relate to your
pain: "If I commit suicide, my parents will know from that
how much I hate them." There's nothing like that here. It is
a nonexistent world, but he is still there, existing with it.

STUDENT: I don't understand this extrahuman quality of
being born out of a lotus plant—like Christ's having a vir-

gin mother. Isn't that presenting Padmasambhava as an ideal beyond us that we have to relate to as other-than-human?

TRUNGPA RINPOCHE: In some way, being born from a mother and from a lotus are exactly the same situation. There is nothing all that superhuman about it: it is an expression of miracles that do exist. People who watch a birth for the first time often find that that is a miracle too. In the same way, being born from a lotus is a miracle, but there is nothing particularly divine or pure about it. Being born from a lotus is an expression of openness. The process of being in the womb for nine months does not have to be gone through. It is a free and open situation—the lotus opens and the child is there. It is a very straightforward thing. With regard to the lotus, we do not have to discuss such questions as the validity of the statement that Christ's mother was a virgin. There could only be this one lotus there at that time. Then it died. So we could say it was a free birth.

S: Birth from the lotus could also mean the negation of karmic history.

TR: That's right, yes. There is no karmic history involved at all. Just somewhere in Afghanistan a lotus happened to bear a child.

STUDENT: Could you please say something about the relationship between the Vajradhara aspect of Padmasambhava and the dharmakaya buddha of the Kagyü lineage, also called Vajradhara?

TRUNGPA RINPOCHE: As you say, for the Kagyü lineage, Vajradhara is the name of the primordial buddha on the dharmakaya level, who is continuously existing. Padmasambhava's Vajradhara aspect is on the sambhogakaya level of relating with life experiences; or on a secondary dharmakaya level it is connected with the all-pervasiveness of sentient beings, there at your disposal to work with. But it is primarily a sambhogakaya principle. In this sense, the five aspects of the sambhogakaya, the five sambhogakaya buddhas, are the eight aspects of Padmasambhava.

STUDENT: You talked about staying with the irritation; in fact, savoring it. Is the idea that pain is associated with withdrawal and avoidance, so you move into the pain or closer to the pain, and it disappears? Is there some possibility of enlightenment coming out of that?

TRUNGPA RINPOCHE: This is actually a very delicate point. We have the problem that a sort of sadistic attitude could occur, which we find in a lot of militant attitudes toward Zen practices as well. We also have the "inspirational" approach of getting into the teachings and ignoring the pain. These attitudes lead to blind confusion. And we find our bodies being abused, not taken care of properly.

In this case, relating with the pain is not quite the sadistic approach or that of militant practice on the one hand, nor is it based on the idea of ignoring the whole thing and spacing out into your mind trip on the other hand. It is something between these two. To begin with, pain is regarded as something quite real, something actually happening. It is not regarded as a doctrinal or philosophical matter. It is simple pain or simple psychological discomfort. You don't move away from the pain, because if you do, you have no resources to work with. You don't get into the pain or inflict pain on yourself, because then you are involved in a suicidal process; you are destroying yourself. So it is somewhere between the two.

STUDENT: How does making a home in the irritations relate to the mandala principle?

TRUNGPA RINPOCHE: That seems to be the mandala already, in itself. Relating with the irritations has the sense of there being all kinds of irritations and infinite further possibilities of them. That *is* a mandala. You are right there. Mandala is a sense of total existence with you in the center. So here you are in the center of irritation. It is very powerful.

STUDENT: In defining *vidyadhara* you talked about scientific knowledge. What does scientific knowledge have to do with Padmasambhava's life?

TRUNGPA RINPOCHE: I am using "scientific knowledge" in the sense of the most accurate knowledge on how to react to situations. The essence of crazy wisdom is that you have no strategized programs or ideals any more at all. You are just open. Whatever students present, you just react accordingly. This is continuously scientific in the sense that it is continuously in accordance with the nature of the elements.

Let the Phenomena Play

WE MAY NOT HAVE THE TIME to go through the rest of
the eight aspects of Padmasambhava at the same pace as we
went through the first two. But our discussion so far has
provided a basic ground for the discussion of the whole process of Padmasambhava's life and his personal expansion.
What I would like to do is try to convey a sense of Padmasambhava that brings all of his aspects together. This is very
hard to do, because the medium of words is limited. Words
do not cover enough of the insight. But we shall do our
best.

We are not talking about Padmasambhava from an external historical point of view or an external mythical one. We
are trying to get at the marrow inside the bone, so to
speak—the instantaneous or embryonic aspect of him and
how he relates to life from that. This is a sacred or tantric
way of seeing Padmasambhava's life, as opposed to accounts
and interpretations that see him purely as a historical or
mythical figure—like King Arthur or someone like that.

The inside story is based on the relationship of the events
in Padmasambhava's life to the teachings. This is the point
of view from which I have been trying to work into the story

of Padmasambhava as the young prince and as the young *siddha*, or accomplished yogi, in the charnel ground. These two aspects are extraordinarily important for the rest of Padmasambhava's life.

Padmasambhava's next phase arose from the need for him to be accepted into the monastic life. He had to be ordained as a *bhikshu*, or monk. Relating with the monastic system was important because it provided a disciplinary situation. Padmasambhava was ordained by Ananda, a disciple and attendant of the Buddha. As a monk, Padmasambhava acquired the name Shakya Simha, or Shakya Senge in Tibetan, which means "Lion of the Shakya Tribe." This was one of the Buddha's names (the Buddha was also sometimes known as "the Sage of the Shakyas"), and through this name Padmasambhava became identified with the tradition of the Buddha. This was very important, because one needs a tremendous sense of relationship with the lineage. So Padmasambhava associated himself with the lineage and realized what an important part it plays.

The lineage of the Buddha is a lineage of constant basic sanity, a sane approach to life. Becoming a monk means living life sanely—sanely and saintly—because it is a complete and total involvement with things as they are. As a monk, you do not miss any points. You relate with life from the point of view that the given moment actually permits a sense of a living quality, a sense of totality, a sense of not being moved by passion, aggression, or anything at all—you are just dealing with things as the monastic life permits, as they are.

As Padmasambhava developed in his monastic role, he again began to manifest in the style of a young prince, but in this case as a young prince who had become a monk. He decided to become the savior of the world, the bringer of the message of dharma.

One day he visited a nunnery. At this particular nunnery lived a princess called Mandarava, who had just recently become a nun and had completely turned away from worldly pleasure. She lived in seclusion, guarded by five hundred women, whose task was to make sure that she maintained her monastic discipline. When Padmasambhava arrived at the monastery, everyone was quite impressed with him— naturally. He had the innocence of one born from a lotus and a pure and ideal physique. He was very beautiful. He converted all the women in the nunnery: they all became his students.

The king, Mandarava's father, soon heard something of this. A cowherd reported that he had heard an unusual male voice coming from the nunnery, preaching and shouting. The king had thought that Mandarava was an absolutely perfect nun and had no relations of any kind with men. He got quite upset at the cowherd's news and sent his ministers to find out what was happening at the nunnery. The ministers were not allowed into the nunnery compound but suspected that something funny was going on there. They reported back to the king, who decided to have the army destroy the nunnery gate, march in, and arrest this rascal posing as a teacher. This they did. They captured Padmasambhava and put him on a pyre of sandalwood and set it afire (this was the style of execution that had developed in that particular kingdom). The princess was thrown into some pitch containing thorns and lice and fleas. This was the king's idea of religion.

The fire in which Padmasambhava had been placed burned on and on, for seven days. Usually when they executed someone, the fire lasted only for a day or two. In this case, however, it burned on and on. Very unusual. The king began to think that perhaps there was also something unusual about this man wandering about pretending to be a guru.

He sent his men to investigate, and they found that the fire had disappeared and that the whole area where the fire had been had turned into a huge lake. In the middle of the lake was Padmasambhava, once again sitting on a lotus. When the king heard this, he decided to find out more about this person. He decided not to trust the matter to a messenger, but went himself to see Padmasambhava. When he arrived at the scene, he was overwhelmed by the presence of this person sitting on a lotus in the middle of a lake where a charnel ground and a place to burn criminals had been. The king confessed his wrongdoings and foolish actions to Padmasambhava and invited him back to the palace. Padmasambhava refused to go, saying he would not enter the palace of a sinner—the palace of a wicked king who had condemned someone who was the spiritual essence of both king and guru, who had ignored the true essence of spirituality. The king repeated his request and finally Padmasambhava accepted his invitation. The king himself pulled the car in which Padmasambhava sat. Padmasambhava became the *rajguru,* the king's guru, and Mandarava was rescued from the pitch.

During this phase of his life, Padmasambhava's approach to reality was one of accuracy, but within this realm of accuracy he was ready to allow people room to make mistakes on the spiritual path. He was even ready to go so far as to let the king try to burn him alive and put his student, the princess, into the pitch. He felt he should let those things happen. This is an important point that already shows the pattern of his teaching.

There had to be room for the king's realization of his neurosis—his whole way of acting and thinking—to come through by itself. His realization had to be allowed to come through by itself, rather than by Padmasambhava's performing some miraculous act of magical power (which he was quite capable of) before he was arrested. Padmasambhava could have said: "I am the world's greatest teacher; you cannot touch me. Now you will see the greatness of my spiritual power." But he didn't do that. Instead he let himself be arrested.

This is a very important indication of Padmasambhava's way of relating with samsaric, or confused, mind: let the confusion come through, and then let the confusion correct itself. It is like the story about a particular Zen master who had a woman student. The woman became pregnant and bore a child. Her parents came to the Zen master, bringing the child, and complained to him, saying, "This is your child; you should take care of it." The Zen master replied, "Is that so?" and he took the child and cared for it. A few years later, the woman was no longer able to bear the lie she had told—the father of the child was not the teacher but someone else altogether. She went to her parents and said, "My teacher was not the father of the child; it was someone else." Then the parents became worried and felt they had better rescue the child from the hands of the teacher, who was meditating in the mountains. They found him and said: "We have discovered that this is not your child. Now we are going to rescue it from you; we are going to take it away from you. You are not the real father." And the Zen master just said, "Is that so?"

So let the phenomena play. Let the phenomena make fools of themselves by themselves. This is the approach. There is no point in saying: "Let me have a word with you. I would like to explain the whole situation inside-out." By itself, just saying something is inadequate—not to mention the difficulty of finding the right thing to say. It simply does not work. The phenomenal world cannot be conned with words, with logic, petty logic. The phenomenal world can only be dealt with in terms of what happens within it, in terms of its own logic. This is a larger version of the logic, the totality of the logicalness of the situation. So an important feature of Padmasambhava's style is letting the phenomena play themselves through rather than trying to prove or explain something.

In the next situation, the next aspect, Padmasambhava was faced with five hundred heretics, or *tirthikas* in Sanskrit. In this case the heretics were the theists, the Brahmanists; they could also have been Jehovists—or whatever you would like to call the approach that is the opposite of the nontheistic approach of the buddhadharma. A logical debate took place: a huge crowd surrounded two pandits, facing each other. The theistic pandit and the nontheistic pandit were debating each other on the nature of spirituality. Both of them were on a spiritual trip. (It does not matter whether you are a theist or a nontheist—you can still be on a spiritual trip.) Both were trying to establish their territory, to prove that they had grounds for having the spiritual path their way. In this case, the theists won and the Buddhists, who were completely overwhelmed by logical intelligence, lost. Then Padmasambhava was asked to perform a ceremony of destruction, to destroy the theists and their whole setup. He performed the ceremony and caused a huge landslide, which killed the five hundred pandits and destroyed their whole ashram.

In this aspect, Padmasambhava is known as Senge Dradrok, which is "Lion's Roar." The lion's roar destroys the dualistic psychology in which value and validity are attributed to things *because there is the other thing happening*—the Brahma, or God, or whatever you like to call it. The dualistic approach says that because "that" happened, therefore "this" also is a solid and real thing. In order to become Him or Her, whichever it may be, we should be receptive to that higher thing, that objective thing. This approach is always problematic. And the only way to destroy that dualistic setup is to arouse Padmasambhava's crazy-wisdom aspect to destroy it.

From the point of view of crazy wisdom, "that" does not exist; and the reason "that" does not exist is because "this," the self, no longer exists. In some sense, you could say that here the destruction is mutual destruction. But at the same time, this destruction is favorable from the nontheistic point of view. If Jehovah or Brahma exists, then the perceiver has to exist in order to acknowledge that existence. But the crazy-wisdom approach is that the acknowledger does not exist; it is no longer there, or at least it is questionable. And if "this" does not exist, then "that" is out of the question altogether. It is purely a phantom, imaginary. And even for an imagination to exist, you need an imagin*er*. So the destruction of the centralized notion of a self brings with it the nonexistence of "that."

This is the approach of Padmasambhava as Sengye Dradrok, Lion's Roar. The lion's roar is heard, because the lion is not afraid of "that"; the lion is willing to go into, to overwhelm, whatever there is, because "this" does not exist to be destroyed any more. In this sense, the lion's roar can be connected with the development of *vajra pride.*

The next aspect is Dorje Trolö, which came about when Padmasambhava went to Tibet. The Tibetans were not involved in foreign, that is, external, worship. They did not have the Hindu realm of the gods. They did not even know the word *Brahma.* What they had was *yeshen,* which is the equivalent word in the Pön tradition to "absoluteness."[1] *Ye* means "primordial"; *shen* means "ancestralness" or "great friend." In coming to Tibet, the buddhadharma was now encountering an entirely new angle, a new approach.

Up until that time, Padmasambhava had been dealing with Hindus, Brahmanists. What he encountered in Tibet was entirely different from that. The classical Tibetan word *yeshen* has a sense that is something like "ancestral" or "ancient" or even "celestial." It is similar to the Japanese word *shin*, which means "heaven"; or to the Chinese word *ta*, which means "that which is above." All three terms relate to something greater, something above. There is an upward process involved, which could be associated with dragons, thunderstorms, clouds, the sun and moon, stars, and so forth. They relate to that "above" thing, to that higher, greater cosmic pattern.

This was extremely difficult for Padmasambhava to deal with. It was impossible to deal with it through logic, because the wisdom of the Pön tradition was very profound, extremely profound. If Padmasambhava had had to challenge the Pönists with logic, the only approach he could have taken would have been to say that earth and heaven are a unity, that heaven as such does not exist because heaven and earth are interdependent. But that is very shaky logic, because everyone knows that there is earth and there is heaven, that there are mountains and stars and suns and moons. You could not challenge these people by saying that there is no earth, no mountains; there is no sun, no moon, no sky, no stars.

The basic Pön philosophy is very powerful; it is much like the American Indian, Shinto, or Taoist approach to cosmic sanity. The whole thing is an extraordinarily sane approach. But there is a problem. It is also a very anthropocentric approach. The world is created for human beings; animals are human beings' next meal or their skins are human beings' next clothes. This anthropocentic approach is actually lacking in basic sanity; it is not able to respect the basic continuity of consciousness. Consequently, the Pön religion prescribes animal sacrifice to the *yeshen*, or great god. Here again we find a similarity with the American Indian and Shinto outlook, with man as the center of the universe. According to that outlook, the grasses and trees, the wild animals, and the sun and the moon are there for human entertainment. The whole system is based on human existence. That is the big problem.

Buddhism is not a national religious approach. National religions tend to be theistic. Let us remember that Christianity inherited its theistic approach from Judaism; Judaism, Shintoism, Hinduism, and many other religions like them are national religions that are also theistic. They have their particular sense of the relationship between "this" and "that," earth and heaven. The nontheistic approach is extremely difficult to present in a primitive country that already has a belief in a theistic religion. The way the people of such a country relate to their basic survival already contains a sense of the earth in relation to the magnificence of heaven. Their sense of worship is already developed.

Jesuits and other Catholic missionaries have recently developed a method in which they tell primitive peoples, "Yes, your gods do exist, it is true, but my god is much wiser than your god, because it is omnipresent and so forth—ambidextrous and all the rest." But Buddhism faces an entirely different problem. There is no question of your god and my god. You have your god, but I don't have a god, so I am left just sort of suspended there. I have nothing to substitute. Where is the greatness and power of my approach? I have nothing to substitute. The only thing there is to substitute is crazy wisdom—*mind* is very powerful. We all have mind, including animals. Everybody has mind. It does not matter about Him or Them, or Them and Him, or whatever.

One's state of mind is very powerful. It can imagine destroying something, and it destroys it. It can imagine creating something, and it creates it. Whatever you intend in the realm of mind, it happens. Imagine your enemy. You want to destroy your enemy, and you have developed all kinds of tactics for doing so. You have infinite imaginations about how to handle the destruction of that enemy. Imagine your friend. You have infinite inspirations about how to relate with your friend, how to make him or her feel good or better or richer.

That is why we have built these houses and roads, manufactured these beds and blankets. That is why we have provided this food, thought up all kinds of dishes. We have done all this to prove to ourselves that we do exist. This is a kind of humanistic approach. Man does exist, his intelligence does exist. This is entirely nontheistic.

Padmasambhava's approach to magic was on this nontheistic level. Lightning happens because it does happen, rather than because there is any further why or who or what involved. It does happen. Flowers blossom because it happens, it is so. We cannot argue that there are no flowers. We cannot argue that no snow falls. It is so. It happens. It came from up there, from the sky, but so what!? What do you want to manufacture there?

Everything happens on this plane, on this really earthy plane. Everything happens on a very straight and down-to-earth level. Therefore, the crazy wisdom of Dorje Trolö begins to develop. It is extraordinarily powerful. It is powerful on the kitchen-sink level—that is what is so irritating. In fact, that is what is so powerful. It haunts everywhere—it really *is* there.

Dorje Trolö arrives in Tibet riding a pregnant tigress. The tigress is electric. She is pregnant electricity. She is somewhat domesticated, but at the same time has the potential of running wild. Dorje Trolö knows no logic. As far as Dorje Trolö is concerned, the only conventional logic there is is relating with heaven and earth. Because the sky forms itself into its particular shape, the horizon exists. There is the vastness of space, the sky; and there is the vastness of the earth. They are vast, but okay—so what? Do you want to make a big deal out of the vastness? Who are you trying to compete with? There is this vastness, but why not consider the smallest things that are happening as well? Aren't they more threatening? The grain of sand is more threatening than the vastness of space or of the desert; because of its concentratedness, it is extremely explosive. There is a huge cosmic joke here, a gigantic cosmic joke, a very powerful one.

As Dorje Trolö's crazy wisdom expanded, he developed an approach for communicating with future generations. In relation to a lot of his writings, he thought, "These words may not be important at this point, but I am going to write them down and bury them in the mountains of Tibet." And he did so. He thought: "Someone will discover them later and find them extraordinarily mind-blowing. Let them have a good time then." This was a unique approach. Gurus nowadays think purely in terms of the effect they might have now. They do not consider trying to have a powerful effect on the future. But Dorje Trolö thought, "If I leave an example of my teaching behind, even if people of future generations do not experience my example, just hearing my words alone could cause a spiritual atomic bomb to explode in a future time." Such an idea was unheard-of. It is a very powerful thing.

The spiritual force of Padmasambhava as expressed in his manifestation as Dorje Trolö is a direct message that no longer knows any question. It just happens. There is no room for interpretations. There is no room for making a home out of this. There is just spiritual energy going on that is real dynamite. If you distort it, you are destroyed on the spot. If you are actually able to see it, then you are right there with it. It is ruthless. At the same time, it is compassionate, because it has all this energy in it. The pride of being in the state of crazy wisdom is tremendous. But there is a loving quality in it as well.

Can you imagine being hit by love and hate at the same time? In crazy wisdom, we are hit with compassion and wisdom at the same time, without a chance of analyzing them. There's no time to think; there's no time to work things out at all. It is *there*—but at the same time, it isn't there. And at the same time also, it is a big joke.

STUDENT: Does crazy wisdom require raising your energy level?

TRUNGPA RINPOCHE: I don't think so, because energy comes along with the situation itself. In other words, the highway is the energy, not your driving fast. The highway suggests your driving fast. The self-existing energy is there.

S: You're not worried about the car?

TR: No.

STUDENT: Has the crazy-wisdom teaching developed in any lineages other than the Nyingma lineage?

TRUNGPA RINPOCHE: I don't think so. There is also the *mahamudra* lineage, which is based on a sense of precision and accuracy. But the crazy-wisdom lineage that I received from my guru seems to have much more potency. It is somewhat illogical—some people might find the sense of not knowing how to relate with it quite threatening. It seems to be connected with the Nyingma tradition and the *maha ati* lineage exclusively.

STUDENT: What was the name of the Padmasambhava aspect before Dorje Trolö?

TRUNGPA RINPOCHE: Nyima Öser, "Holding the Sun."

S: Was that when he was with Mandarava?

TR: No. Then he was known as Loden Choksi. In the iconography, he is wearing a white turban.

STUDENT: Are there any controls or precepts connected with crazy wisdom?

TRUNGPA RINPOCHE: Other than itself, there doesn't seem to be anything. Just being itself.

S: There are no guidelines?

TR: There is no textbook for becoming a crazy-wisdom person. It doesn't hurt to read books, but unless you are able to have some experience of crazy wisdom yourself through contact with the crazy-wisdom lineage—with somebody who is crazy and wise at the same time—you won't get much out of books alone. A lot really depends on the lineage message, on the fact that somebody has already inherited something. Without that, the whole thing becomes purely mythical. But if you see that somebody does possess some element of crazy wisdom, that will provide a certain reassurance, which is worthwhile at this point.

STUDENT: Could you mention one of the spiritual time bombs, other than the lineage itself, that was left behind by Padmasambhava as a legacy and as a teaching that is relevant today?

TRUNGPA RINPOCHE: We might say this seminar is one of them. If we weren't interested in Padmasambhava, we wouldn't be here. He left his legacy, his personality, behind, and that is why we are here.

STUDENT: You mentioned some of the difficulties Padmasambhava faced in presenting the dharma to the Tibetans, principally that the Tibetans' mental outlook was theistic while Buddhism is nontheistic. What are the difficulties in presenting the dharma to the Americans?

TRUNGPA RINPOCHE: I think it is the same thing. The Americans worship the sun and the water gods and the mountain gods—they still do. That is a very primordial approach, and some Americans are rediscovering their heritage. We have people going on an American Indian trip, which is beautiful, but the knowledge we have of it is not all that accurate. Americans regard themselves as sophisticated and scientific, as educated experts on everything. But still we are actually on the level of ape culture. Padmasambhava's approach of crazy wisdom is further education for us—we could become transcendental apes.

STUDENT: Could you say something more about vajra pride?

TRUNGPA RINPOCHE: Vajra pride is the sense that basic sanity does exist in our state of being, so we don't particularly have to try to work it out logically. We don't have to prove that something is happening or not happening. The basic dissatisfaction that causes us to look for some spiritual understanding is an expression of vajra pride: we are not willing to submit to the suppression of our confusion. We are willing to stick our necks out. That seems to be a first expression of the vajra-pride instinct—and we can go on from there!

STUDENT: Two of the aspects of Padmasambhava seem to be contradictory. Padmasambhava allowed the confusion of the king to manifest and then turn back on itself, yet he didn't allow the confusion of the five hundred pandits to manifest (if you want to call dualism confusion). He just destroyed them with a landslide. Could you comment on this?

TRUNGPA RINPOCHE: The pandits seem to have been very simple-minded people, because they had no connection with the kitchen-sink-level problems of life. They were purely thriving on their projection of who they were. So, according to the story, the only way to relate with them was to provide them with the experience of the landslide—a sudden jerk or shock. Anything else they could have reinterpreted into something else. If the pandits had been in the king's situation, they would have been much more hardened, much less enlightened, than he was. They had no willingness to relate with anything at all, because they were so hardened in their dogmatism. Moreover, it was necessary for them to realize the nonexistence of themselves and Brahma. So they were provided with the experience of a catastrophe that was caused not by Brahma but by themselves. This left them in a nontheistic situation: they themselves were all that there was; there was no possibility of reproaching God or Brahma or whatever.

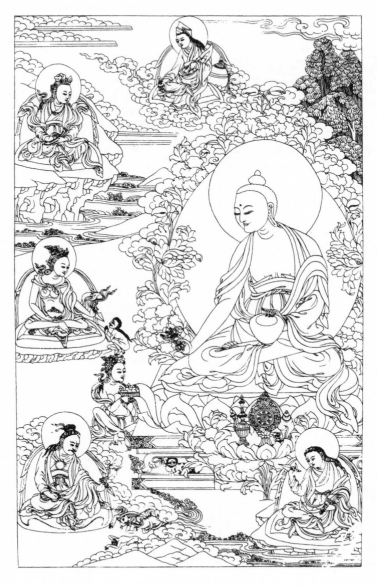

Shakya Senge

6

Cynicism and Devotion

HOPEFULLY you have had at least a glimpse of Padmasambhava and his aspects. According to tradition, there are three
ways in which the life of Padmasambhava can be told: the
external, factual way; the internal, psychological way; and
the higher, secret way, which is the approach of crazy wisdom. We have concentrated on the secret way, with some elements of the other two.

By way of conclusion, it would be good to discuss how we
can relate with Padmasambhava. Here we are considering
Padmasambhava as a cosmic principle rather than as a historical person, an Indian saint. Different manifestations of this
principle appear constantly: Padmasambhava is Shakya
Senge, the yogi Nyima Öser, the prince Pema Gyalpo, the
mad yogi Dorje Trolö, and so forth. The Padmasambhava
principle contains every element that is part of the enlightened world.

Among my students, a particular approach to the teachings seems to have developed. By way of beginning, we have
adopted an attitude of distrust: distrust toward ourselves and
also toward the teachings and the teacher—toward the whole
situation in fact. We feel that everything should be taken

with a grain of salt, that we should examine and test everything thoroughly to make sure it is good gold. In taking
this approach, we have had to develop our sense of hon-
esty—we have to cut through our own self-deceptions, which
play an important part. We cannot establish spirituality
without cutting through spiritual materialism.

Having already prepared the basic ground with the help of
this distrust, it may be time to change gears, so to speak,
and try almost the opposite approach. Having developed accurate and vajralike cynicism and having cultivated vajra nature, we could begin to realize what spirituality is. And we
find that spirituality is completely ordinary. It is completely
ordinary ordinariness. Though we might speak of it as extraordinary, in fact it is the most ordinary thing of all.

To relate with this, we might have to change our pattern.
The next step is to develop devotion and faith. We cannot
relate to the Padmasambhava principle unless there is some
kind of warmth. If we cut through deception completely and
honestly, then a positive situation begins to develop. We
gain a positive understanding of ourselves as well as of the
teachings and the teacher. In order to work with the grace,
or *adhishthana,* of Padmasambhava, with this cosmic principle of basic sanity, we have to develop a kind of romanticism. This is equally important as the cynical approach we
have been taking up till now.

There are two types of this romantic, or *bhakti,* approach.
One is based on a sense of poverty. You feel you don't have
it, but the others do. You admire the richness of "that": the
goal, the guru, the teachings. This is a poverty approach—
you feel that these other things are so beautiful because you
don't have what they have. It is a materialistic approach—
that of spiritual materialism—and it is based on there not
being enough sanity in the first place, not enough sense of
confidence and richness.

The other type of romantic approach is based on the sense that you do have it; it is there already. You do not admire it because it is somebody else's, because it is somewhere far away, distant from you, but because it is right near—in your heart. It is a sense of appreciation of what you are. You have as much as the teacher has, and you are on the path of dharma yourself, so you do not have to look at the dharma from outside. This is a sane approach; it is fundamentally rich; there is no sense of poverty at all.

This type of romanticism is important. It is the most powerful thing of all. It cuts through cynicism, which exists purely for its own sake, for the sake of its own protection. It cuts through cynicism's ego game and develops further and greater pride—vajra pride, as it is called. There is a sense of beauty and even of love and light. Without this, relating with the Padmasambhava principle is purely a matter of seeing how deep and profound you can get in your psychological experience. It remains a myth, something that you do not have; therefore it sounds interesting but never becomes personal. Devotion or compassion is the only way of relating with the grace—the adhishthana, or blessing—of Padmasambhava.

It seems that many people find this cynical and skeptical style that we have developed so far too irritatingly cold. Particularly people who are having their first encounter with our scene say this. There is no sense of invitation; people are constantly being scrutinized and looked down upon. Maybe that is a very honest way for you to relate with the "other," which is also you. But at some point, some warmth has to develop in addition to the coldness. You do not exactly have to change the temperature—intense coldness *is* warmth—but there is a certain twist we could accomplish. It lies only in our conceptual mind and logic. In reality there is no twist at all, but we have to have some way of putting this into words. What we are talking about is irritatingly warm and so powerful, so magnetizing.

So our discussion of Padmasambhava seems to be a landmark in the geography of our journey together. It is time to begin with that romantic approach, if we may call it that: the sane romantic approach, not the materialistic romantic approach.

Our seminar here happened purely by accident, even though it involved a lot of organizing, working a lot of things out. But still it was worked out accidentally. It is a very precious accident that we were able to discuss such a topic as the life of Padmasambhava. The opportunity to discuss such a subject is very rare, unique, very precious. But such a rare and precious situation goes on constantly; our life as part of the teachings is extremely precious. Each person came here purely by accident, and since it was an accident, it cannot be repeated. That is why it is precious. That is why the dharma is precious. Everything becomes precious; human life becomes precious.

There is this rare preciousness of our human life: we each have our brain, our sense perceptions, our materials to work on. We have each had our problems in the past: our depressions, our moments of insanity, our struggles—all these make sense. So the journey goes on, the accident goes on— which is that we are here. This is the kind of romanticism, the kind of warmth I am talking about. It is worthwhile approaching the teaching in this way. If we do not, we cannot relate with the Padmasambhava principle.

STUDENT: Could you tell us something about how you related to the crazy wisdom of your guru Jamgön Kongtrül of Sechen, if he had it, and how you combined those two approaches of wealth and poverty when you studied with him?

TRUNGPA RINPOCHE: I think my way of working with it

was very similar to everyone else's. At the beginning, personally, I had a lot of fascination and admiration based on the poverty point of view. Also it was very exciting, because seeing Jamgön Kongtrül Rinpoche rather than just having to sit and memorize texts provided quite a break. It was always fun to watch him, and to hang out with him was great.

This was still based on a poverty-stricken kind of mentality—on being entertained by that which you do not have. All I had were my books to read and my tutor to discipline me. Moreover, Jamgön Kongtrül, with his extraordinary understanding and spiritual energy, was presented as the example of what I should become when I grew up. This is what I was told over and over again, which was based on the style of poverty and materialism. Of course, the people in the monastery cared for me, but they were also concerned with public relations: fame, glory, enlightenment.

But as I became close to Jamgön Kongtrül, I gradually stopped trying to collect something for myself so that I could be enriched. I began just to enjoy his presence, just to go along with him. Then I could really feel his warmth and his richness and be part of it as well. So it seems that you start with the materialistic approach and gradually change to the sane approach, to devotion.

As far as Jamgön Kongtrül is concerned, he possessed all the qualities of Padmasambhava. Sometimes he looked just like a big baby. That was the little prince aspect. Sometimes he was kind and helpful. Sometimes he put out black air that gave you the feeling that something was wrong and made you feel extraordinarily paranoid. I used to feel like I had a huge head hanging out and was very embarrassed about it, but I didn't know what to do.

STUDENT: Is the cynical phase that we have been going through due to our being Americans? Does it have something to do with American culture, or has it got to do with something about the teachings that is independent of culture?

TRUNGPA RINPOCHE: I think it is both. It is because of American culture, especially because of this particular period of social change in which a spiritual supermarket has developed. So we have to be smart to beat the supermarket mentality, to not be sucked in by it.

On the other hand, it is also a very Buddhistic approach. You can imagine finding this kind of mentality at Nalanda University. Naropa and all the other pandits were cutting through everything with their superlogical minds. It was quite awesome. This approach is connected with the Buddhist idea that the teachings begin with pain and suffering. This is the First Noble Truth. It is a realistic way of looking at things. It is not enough just to be simple-minded and malleable; some weight is needed; some cynicism. Then by the time you get to talking about the path, which is the Fourth Noble Truth, you have the sense of something positive coming out, which is the devotional part coming through.

So it is a combination of cultural and inherent factors. Still, that is the way it ought to begin. And it does begin that way.

STUDENT: You used the word *accident*. In your view, does that include free will?

TRUNGPA RINPOCHE: Well, it's both; that is, free will is the cause of the accident. Without free will, you can't have accident.

STUDENT: We have been talking about Padmasambhava's way of relating to confused people. Do you think it's appropriate to take the viewpoint of Padmasambhava in relating to ourselves; for example, should we let the neurosis flood in and things like that?

TRUNGPA RINPOCHE: I think that is the whole point, yes. There is a Padmasambhava aspect in us. There are certain tendencies not to accept our existing confusion and to want to cut through it. There is something in us that says we are not subject to the confusion, a revolutionary aspect.

STUDENT: Is it important to try to avoid cynicism now in our approach to the teachings?

TRUNGPA RINPOCHE: I think the cynicism remains continuous and becomes powerful cynicism. You cannot just switch it on and off like changing television channels. It has to continue, and it should be there. For instance, when you encounter a new or further level of teaching, you should test it out in the same way as you have been doing. Then you will have more information and your eventual trust in it will have more backbone.

STUDENT: Does Padmasambhava's teaching remain up to date? Don't historical and cultural changes require changes in the teaching?

TRUNGPA RINPOCHE: It remains up to date because it is based on relating with confusion. Our confusion remains up to date, otherwise it would not confuse us. And the realization of confusion also remains up to date, because confusion causes our question and prompts us to wake up. The realization of the confusion is the teaching, so it is a constantly living situation, constantly lived-in and always applicable.

STUDENT: You spoke earlier about Padmasambhava being in a state of decisionlessness. Is that the same thing as not thinking at all? You know—the mind just functioning?

TRUNGPA RINPOCHE: Which is thinking. But you *can*

think without thinking. There is a certain kind of intelligence connected with the totality that is more precise, but it is not verbal; it is not conceptualized at all. It does think in some sense, but it is not thinking in the ordinary sense.

S: Is it thinking without scheming?

TR: Something more than that. It *is* thinking without scheming, but it is still something more than that. It is a self-existing intelligence of its own.

STUDENT: Rinpoche, about devotion. I can become so joyous when I experience the dharma's living quality. There's such great joy; it's like being high. But then I find a fall can follow this experience, which brings me down to a sort of barren land or desolate country. I've been feeling it's better to avoid these extreme feelings, because they seem always to bring their opposite.

TRUNGPA RINPOCHE: You see, if your approach is a poverty approach, then it is like begging for food. You're given food and you enjoy it while you're eating it. But then you have to beg again, and between the two beggings there is a very undesirable state. It's that kind of thing. It's still relating to the dharma as the "other," rather than feeling that you have it. Once you realize that the dharma is you and you are in it already, you don't feel particularly joyous. There is no extra bliss or any high of any kind at all. If you are high, then you are high all the time, so there is no reference point for comparison. And if you are not high, then you are extraordinarily ordinary.

STUDENT: Doesn't your idea of accident contradict the law of karma, which is that everything has a cause and effect?

TRUNGPA RINPOCHE: Accident is karma. Karmic situations take place by way of accident. It works like flint and steel coming together and causing a spark. Events come unexpectedly. Any event is always a sudden event, but it is a karmic one. The original idea of karma is the evolutionary action of the twelve *nidanas,* which begins with ignorance, with the potter's wheel. That evolutionary action that begins with ignorance is an accident.

S: The ignorance itself is the accident?

TR: Ignorance itself is the accident. Duality itself is the accident. It is a big misunderstanding.

Crazy Wisdom Seminar II

KARME-CHÖLING 1972

Pema Jungne

I

Padmasambhava and the Energy of Tantra

IN THIS SEMINAR, we will be studying Tibet's great Buddhist saint Padmasambhava. Padmasambhava was the great Indian yogi and vidyadhara who introduced the complete teachings of buddhadharma to Tibet, including the vajrayana, or tantra. As to the dates and historical details, we are uncertain. Padmasambhava is supposed to have been born twelve years after the death of the Buddha. He continued to live and went to Tibet in the eighth century to propagate the buddhadharma there. Our approach here, as far as chronology and such things are concerned, is entirely unscholastic. For those of you who are concerned with dates and other such historical facts and figures, I am afraid I will be unable to furnish accurate data. Nevertheless, the inspiration of Padmasambhava, however old or young he may be, goes on.

Rather than studying the life and acts of Padmasambhava according to a chronological-historical description, we will be trying to discuss the fundamental meaning of Padmasambhava-ism, if you wish to call it that—the basic qualities of Padmasambhava's existence as they are connected with the dawn of the vajrayana teachings in Tibet. We might call this the Padmasambhava principle. The Padmasambhava principle opened the minds of millions of people in Tibet and is already opening peoples' minds in this country, and in the rest of the world for that matter.

Padmasambhava's function in Tibet was to bring forth the teachings of the Buddha by relating with the Tibetan barbarians. The Tibetans of those times believed in a self and a higher authority outside the self, which is known as God. Padmasambhava's function was to destroy those beliefs. His approach was: if there is no belief in the self, then there is no belief in God—a purely nontheistic approach, I am afraid. He had to destroy those nonexistent sand castles that we build. So the significance of Padmasambhava is connected with the destruction of those delusive beliefs. His entry into Tibet meant the destruction of the delusive theistic spiritual structures that had been established in that country. Padmasambhava came to Tibet and introduced Buddhism. In the course of introducing it, he discovered that he not only had to destroy people's primitive beliefs, but he also had to raise their consciousness at the same time. So in introducing the Padmasambhava principle here, we must also relate with the same basic problems of destroying what has to be destroyed and cultivating what has to be cultivated.

To begin with, we have to destroy certain fallacious notions connected with holiness, spirituality, goodness, heaven, godhood, and so forth. What makes these fallacious is the belief in a self, ego. That belief makes it so that *I* am practicing goodness; thus goodness is separated from me; or it implies some kind of a relationship in which goodness depends on me and me depends on goodness. Thus, fundamentally [since neither exists on its own], there is nothing there to build on at all. With this ego approach, a conclusion is drawn because of "other" factors that prove that the conclusion is so. From that point of view, we are building sand castles, or building castles on an ice block.

According to the Buddhist outlook, ego, or self, is nonexistent. It is not founded on any definite, real factors at all. It is based purely on the belief or assumption that since I call myself so-and-so, therefore I exist. And if I do not know what I am called, what my name is, then there is no structure there on which the whole thing is based. The way this primitive belief works is that believing in "that," the other, brings "this," the self. If "that" exists, then "this" must also exist. I believe in "that" because I need a reference point for my own existence, for "this."

In the tantric, or vajrayana, approach introduced into Tibet by Padmasambhava, my existence in relationship with others who exist is based on some energy. It is founded on some sense of understanding, which could also equally well be some sense of misunderstanding.

When we ask ourselves "Who are you, what are you?" and we answer "I am so-and-so," our affirmation or confirmation is based on putting something into that empty question. A question is like a container that we put something into to make it an appropriate and valid container. There is some energy that is there between the two processes of giving birth to a question and producing an answer, an energy process that develops at the same time. The energy that develops between the question and the answer is connected either with complete truth or complete falsehood. Strangely enough, those two do not contradict each other. Complete truth and complete falsehood are in some sense the same thing. They make sense simultaneously. Truth is false, falsehood is true. And that kind of energy, which goes on continuously, is called tantra. Because it does not matter here about logical problems of truth or falsehood, the state of mind connected with this is called crazy wisdom.

What I am trying to say is that always our minds are completely and constantly fixed on relating to things as either yes or no; yes in the sense of existence, no in the sense of disproving that existence. Yet our framework of mind continues all the time between those two attitudes. Yes is based on exactly the same sense of reference point as the negation is.

So the basic framework of mind involving a sense of reference point goes on continuously, which means that there is some energy constantly happening. What this means in terms of our relating to the Padmasambhava principle is that we do not have to negate the experience of our lives. We do not have to negate our materialistic or spiritually materialistic experiences. We do not have to negate them as being bad things; nor for that matter do we have to affirm them as being good things. We could relate to the simultaneous birth into existence of things as they are.[2]

This makes sense because what we are trying to do all the time is fight on that ground or battlefield. We are fighting over who possesses the battlefield, whether the battlefield belongs to the attackers or the defenders, and so forth. But in all this, nobody has ever really discussed whether this battlefield itself actually exists or not. And what we are saying here is that that ground or battlefield does exist. Our negations or affirmations as to whether it belongs to ourselves or the others do not make any difference at all. All the time we are affirming or negating we are standing on this ground anyway. This ground we are standing on is the place of birth as well as the place of death, simultaneously. This provides some sense of solidity as far as the principle of Padmasambhava is concerned.

We are talking about a particular energy that permits the teachings to be transmitted by the Padmasambhava principle. The Padmasambhava principle belongs neither to wickedness nor goodness; it belongs to neither yes nor no. It is a principle that accommodates everything that exists in our life situations altogether. Because that energy exists in people's life situations, the Padmasambhava principle was able to bring the buddhadharma to Tibet. In a sense, the theistic beliefs that existed in Tibet—the belief in self and God as separate and the notion of trying to reach higher realms—did have to be destroyed. Those primitive beliefs had to be destroyed, just as we are doing here. Those primitive beliefs in the separate reality of me and my object of worship have to be destroyed. Unless these dualistic notions are destroyed, there is no starting point for giving birth to tantra. The birth of tantra takes place from the nonexistence of belief in "this" and "that."

But Tibetans were very powerful people when Padmasambhava came. They did not believe in philosophies or any of the cunning things that pandits might say. They did not regard a pandit's cleverness as any kind of credential. The Pön tradition of Tibet was very solid and definite and sane. The Tibetans did not believe in what Padmasambhava had to say philosophically about such things as the transitoriness of ego. They would not make sense out of anything like that at all. They would regard such logical analyses as just purely a collection of riddles—Buddhist riddles.

What the Tibetans believed was that life exists and I exist and my ongoing activities of life—working with the dairy animals, working in the fields—exist. The dairy farm and the fields do exist and my practical activities connected with them are my sacred activities, my *sadhanas*. The Pön outlook is that these things exist because I have to feed my child, I have to milk my cow, I have to grow my crops, I have to make butter and cheese. I believe those simple truths. Our Pön tradition is valid, because it believes in the sacredness of feeding life, bringing forth food from the earth in order to feed our offspring. These very simple things exist. This is religion, this is truth, as far as the Pön tradition is concerned.

This simplicity is similar to what we find in the American Indian tradition. Killing a buffalo is an act of creativity because it feeds the hungry; it also controls the growth of the buffalo herd and in that way, maintains a balance. It is that kind of ecological approach.

We find all kinds of ecological approaches of this type, which are extremely sane and solid. In fact, one might have second thoughts as to whether this country is yet ripe for the presentation of Padmasambhava's wisdom, because some people believe in those ecological philosophies and some do not. Some people are very dogmatic advocates of those ecological philosophies and some have no knowledge of them at all. On account of that, one wonders a bit how to approach this culture. But on the whole, there is a certain continuity in what is happening. There is one basic general approach in this culture: we think that everything exists for our benefit.

For instance, we think the body is extremely important, because it maintains the mind. The mind feeds the body and the body feeds the mind. We feel it is important to keep this happening in a healthy manner for our benefit, and we have come to the conclusion that the easiest way to achieve this tremendous scheme of being healthy is to start with the less complicated side of it: feed the body. Then we can wait and see what happens with the mind. If we are less hungry, then we are more likely to be psychologically jolly, and then we may feel like looking into the teachings of depth psychology or other philosophies.

This is also the approach of the Pön tradition: Let us kill a yak; that will make us spiritually higher. Our bodies will be healthier, so our minds will be higher. American Indians would say, let us kill one buffalo. It is the same logic. It is very sensible. We could not say that it is insane at all. It is extremely sane, extremely realistic, very reasonable and logical. There is a pattern there to be respected, and if you put the pattern into practice in a manner that is worthy of respect, then the pattern will continue and you will achieve your results.

We are involved in that kind of approach in this country as well. A lot of people in this country are into the Red American cult as opposed to the White American cult. As far as the Red American cult is concerned, you have your land, you build your tepee, you relate with your children and grandchildren and great-great-great grandchildren. You have dignity and character. You are not afraid of any threat—you develop warriorlike qualities. Then you consider how to handle your children, how to teach them respect for the nation. You instruct your children properly and you become a solid citizen.

Philosophies of this type are to be found not only among the Red Americans, but also among the Celts, the pre-Christian Scandinavians, and the Greeks and Romans. Such a philosophy can be found in the past of any nation that had a pre-Christian or pre-Buddhist religion, a religion of fertility or ecology—such as that of the Jews, the Celts, the American Indians, whatever. That approach of venerating fertility and relating with the earth still goes on, and it is very powerful and very beautiful. I appreciate it very thoroughly, and I could become a follower of such a philosophy. In fact, I am one. I am a Pönist. I believe in Pön because I am Tibetan.

Believing so much in this makes me think of something else that lies outside this framework that is purely concerned with fertility, which is purely body-oriented, which believes that the body will feed the psychology of higher enlightenment. It makes me have questions about the whole thing. If you have such questions, this does not necessarily mean that you have to give up your previous beliefs. If you are a believer and practitioner of the Red American cult, you do not have to become a White American. The question here is, how does your philosophy relate with the reality of the psychological aspect of life? What do we really mean by "body"? What do we really mean by "mind"? What is the body? What is the mind? The body consists of that which needs to be fed; the mind is that which needs to survey whether the body is fed properly. So needing to be fed is another part of the aggregate of the structure of mind.

The whole problem comes not from having to be fed properly or from having to maintain your health properly; the problem comes from belief in the separateness of "I" and "that." I am separate from my food and my food is not me; therefore, I have to consume that particular food that is not me so that it can become part of me.

In the Pön tradition of Tibet, there was a mystical approach toward overcoming separateness, based on the *advaita* principle, the not-two principle. But even with this, until you became the earth itself or until you became the creator of the world, you could not solve your problem. Certain Pön ceremonies reflect a very primitive level of belief concerning overcoming the separateness. The idea is that we have to create an object of worship and then eat the object of worship—chew it, swallow it. Once we have digested it, we should believe that we are completely *advaita*, not-two. This is something like what happens in the Christian traditional ceremony of Holy Communion. To begin with, there is a separateness between you and God, or you and the Son or the Holy Ghost. You and they are separate entities. Until you have associated yourself with the flesh and blood of Christ, represented by certain materials into which the Holy Ghost enters, then you cannot have complete union with them. You cannot have complete union until you eat the bread and drink the wine. The fact that until you do that you cannot become one shows that this is still an act of separateness. Eating and drinking is destroying the separateness, but fundamentally the separateness is still there; when you shit and piss, you end up with the separateness again. There is a problem there.

The sense of becoming one cannot be based on a physical act of doing something—on taking part in a ceremony in this case. To become one with the reality, I have to give up hope of becoming one with the reality. In other words, in relation to "this" exists and "that" exists, I give up hope. I can't work all this out. I give up hope. I don't care if "that" exists or "this" exists, I give up hope. This hopelessness is the starting point of the process of realization.

As we were flying today from Denver to Boston, we encountered a beautiful sight, a vision if you like. Out the window of the airplane was a ring of light reflected on the clouds, a rainbow that followed us wherever we went. In the center of the rainbow ring, in the distance, there was what seemed to be a little peanut shape, a little shadow. As we began to descend and came closer to the clouds, we realized that the peanut shape was actually the shadow of the airplane surrounded by the ring of the rainbow. It was beautiful, miraculous in fact. As we descended further into the depths of the clouds, the shadow became bigger and bigger. We began to make out the complete shape of the airplane, with the tail, the head, and the wings. Then, just as we were about to land, the rainbow ring disappeared and the shadow disappeared. That was the end of our vision.

This reminded me of when we used to look at the moon on a hazy day and see a rainbow ring around the moon. At some point you realize that it is not you looking at the moon but the moon looking at you. What we saw reflected on the clouds was our own shadow. It is mind-boggling. Who is watching who? Who is tricking who?

The approach of crazy wisdom here is to give up hope. There is no hope of understanding anything at all. There is no hope of finding out who did what or what did what or how anything worked. Give up your ambition to put the jigsaw puzzle together. Give it up altogether, absolutely; throw it up in the air, put it in the fireplace. Unless we give up this hope, this precious hope, there is no way out at all.

It is like trying to work out who is in control of the body or the mind, who has the closest link with God—or who has the closest link with the truth, as the Buddhists would say. Buddhists would say that Buddha had the truth, because he didn't believe in God. He found that the truth is free of God. But the Christians or other theists would say that the truth exists because a truth-maker exists. Fighting out those two polarities seems to be useless at this point. It is a completely hopeless situation, absolutely hopeless. We do not understand—and we have no possibility of understanding—anything at all. It is hopeless to look for something to understand, for something to discover, because there is no discovery at all at the end, unless we manufacture one. But if we did manufacture a discovery, we would not be particularly happy about that later on. Though we would thrive on it, we would know that we had cheated ourselves. We would know that there was some secret game that had gone on between "me" and "that."

So the introductory process of Padmasambhava's crazy wisdom is giving up hope, giving up hope *completely*. Nobody is going to comfort you, and nobody is going to help you. The whole idea of trying to find the root or some logic for the discovery of crazy wisdom is completely hopeless. There is no ground, so there is no hope. There is also no fear, for that matter, but we had better not talk about that too much.

STUDENT: Is this hopelessness the same hopelessness you have talked about in connection with shunyata?

TRUNGPA RINPOCHE: I wouldn't even like to connect it with shunyata. This hopelessness provides no security, not even as much as shunyata.

STUDENT: I don't understand why there's no fear here. It seems there would be a possibility of quite a lot of fear.

TRUNGPA RINPOCHE: You have no hope, how can you have fear? There's nothing to look forward to, so you have nothing to lose.

S: If you have nothing to lose and nothing to gain, why keep on studying? Why not just sit back with a bottle of beer?

TR: Well, that in itself is an act of hope and fear. If you just sit back with a beer and relax, saying to yourself, "Well, now, everything's okay—there's nothing to lose, nothing to gain," that in itself is an act of hopefulness and fearfulness. [It is trying to supply a way out,] but you have no way out.

You see, hopelessness and fearlessness is not release, but further imprisonment. You have trapped yourself into spirituality already. You have created your own spiritual trip, and you are trapped in it. That's the other way of looking at this.

S: So this is like acceptance?

TR: No, I wouldn't say it is anything so philosophical as acceptance. It is more desperate than acceptance.

S: Giving up?

TR: Giving up is desperate. In giving up, you have been squeezed into giving up hope; you haven't requested to give up hope.

STUDENT: It seems that playing on the battlefield of your territory of yes and no is the way, since there is no way out of it.

TRUNGPA RINPOCHE: I wouldn't say it's the way, because that provides some kind of hope.

S: But there's no other battlefield to play on.

TR: Well, that's very hopeless, yes.

STUDENT: A minute ago, you seemed to say that even shunyata could provide a sense of security.

TRUNGPA RINPOCHE: It depends on how you relate with it. [If we relate to shunyata as an answer, it might provide some hope.] Until we realize the true implication of hopelessness, we have no chance of understanding crazy wisdom at all, ladies and gentlemen.

S: You just have to give up hope?

TR: Hope and fear.

STUDENT: It seems that you can't just sit back and do nothing. A certain dissatisfaction arises, and so very naturally hope arises that this dissatisfaction could somehow go away. So hope seems to be a very natural and spontaneous thing.

TRUNGPA RINPOCHE: That's too bad. You don't get anything out of it anyway. That's too bad.

S: Yes, but it comes out of every situation, so I don't see how you can possibly avoid it.

TR: You don't have to avoid it out of being hopeful that

that's the right approach. But too bad. It's very simple. The whole thing's hopeless. When we are trying to figure out who's on first and what's on second, there's no way out. Hopeless!

S: Yes, but history, Buddhism, traditions of all kinds give us hope.

TR: Well, they are based on hopelessness, which is why they give some kind of hope. When you give up hope *completely*, there are hopeful situations. But it's hopeless to try and work this out logically. Absolutely hopeless! It doesn't give us any guidelines or maps. The maps would constantly tell us: "No hope there, no hope there, no hope here, no hope there." Hopeless. That's the *whole* point.

S: Hope means the sense that I can do, I can manipulate— is that right?

TR: Yes, the sense that I can get something out of what I am trying to do.

STUDENT: Is the achievement of hopelessness a one-shot affair, where you suddenly just flip into it—

TRUNGPA RINPOCHE: No. It's not a sudden flash that you are saved by. Absolutely not.

S: So it's something that anybody could have some intuition of at any point.

TR: We all do, always. But even that is not *sacred*.

STUDENT: If there are no maps and no guidelines and it's all hopelessness, is there any function for a teacher on this whole trip besides telling you that it's hopeless?

TRUNGPA RINPOCHE: You said it!

STUDENT: Would you advise just diving into the hopelessness or cultivating it little by little?

TRUNGPA RINPOCHE: It's up to you. It's really up to you. I will say one thing. It's impossible to develop crazy wisdom without a sense of hopelessness, *total* hopelessness.

S: Does that mean becoming a professional pessimist?

TR: No, no. A professional pessimist is also hopeful, because he has developed his system of pessimism. It's that same old hopefulness.

STUDENT: What does hopelessness feel like?

TRUNGPA RINPOCHE: Just purely hopeless. No ground, absolutely no ground.

S: The moment you become conscious that you're feeling hopeless, does the hopelessness sort of lose its genuineness?

TR: That depends on whether you regard hopelessness as something sacred according to a religion or spiritual teaching, or whether you regard it as utterly hopeless. That's purely up to you.

S: I mean, we're always talking about this hopelessness, and everybody's beginning to feel that that's the key, so we want it. We feel hopeless and we say, "Well, now I'm on my way." That might eliminate some of the reality of it.

TR: Too bad. Too bad. If you regard it as the path in the sense that you feel you are going to get something out of this, that won't work. There's no way out. That approach is self-defeating. Hopelessness is not a gimmick. It means it, you know; it's the truth. It's the truth of hopelessness, rather than the doctrine of hopelessness.

STUDENT: Rinpoche, if that's so about hopelessness, then the whole picture that we have about the hinayana, mahayana, and vajrayana, and so on, seems to become just a big trip leading to giving up hope. You often talk of a kind of judo practice, using the energy of ego to let it defeat itself.

Here we would somehow use the energy of hope to bring hopelessness, the energy of all this to defeat itself. Is that for real, or is this whole idea of judo practice also just part of the trip?

TRUNGPA RINPOCHE: It is said that at the end of the journey though the nine *yanas*, it is clear that the journey need never have been made. So the path that is presented to us is an act of hopelessness in some sense. The journey need never be made at all. It's eating your own tail and continuing until you eat your own mouth. That's the kind of analogy we could use.

S: It seems that to proceed you have to disregard the warning. Although I may hear that it's hopeless, the only way I can go on at this point is with hope. Why sit and meditate right now? Why not just go out and play? It seems that everything in this situation is a paradox, but, you know, okay, so I'll be here. Even though I hear it's hopeless, I'll pretend.

TR: That's a hopeful act as well, which is in itself hopeless. It eats itself right up. In other words, you think you are able to deceive the path by being a smart traveler on the path, but you begin to realize that you are the path itself. You can't deceive the path, because you make the path. So you're inevitably going to get a very strong message of hopelessness.

S: The only way to get that, it seems, is to keep playing the game.

TR: That's up to you. You could also give up. You have a very definite choice. You have two very definite alternatives, which I suppose we could call sudden enlightenment or gradual enlightenment. This is entirely dependent upon you, on whether you give up hope on the spot or whether you go on playing the game and improvising all kinds of other entertainments. So the sooner you give up hope the better.

STUDENT: It seems that you can put up with a hopeless situation only so long. At a certain point, you just can't relate to it any more and will take advantage of any distraction to turn away from it.

TRUNGPA RINPOCHE: It's up to you.

S: Should you just force yourself again and again, continually, to—

TR: Well, it comes about that way as your life situation goes on.

STUDENT: If the whole situation is hopeless, on what basis do you make decisions like whether to kill one buffalo to feed your family or five hundred buffalo to have their heads on the wall?

TRUNGPA RINPOCHE: Both alternatives are hopeless. Both are ways of trying to survive, which is hope. So both are equally hopeless. We have to learn to work with hopelessness. Nontheistic religion is a hopeless approach of not believing anything. And theistic religion is hopeful, believing in the separateness of me and the nipple I suck on, so to speak. Sorry to be crude, but roughly it works that way.

STUDENT: You said there's no God, there's no self. Is there any so-called true self? Is there anything outside of hopelessness?

TRUNGPA RINPOCHE: I should remind you that this whole thing is the preparation for crazy wisdom, which does not know any kind of truth other than itself. From that point of view, there's no true self, because when you talk about true self or buddha-nature, then that in itself is trying to insert some positive attitude, something to the effect that you are okay. That doesn't exist in this hopelessness.

STUDENT: This hopelessness seems to me to be a restatement of the idea of stopping self-protection, stopping a sense of trying to improve the situation. According to our stereotyped understanding of enlightenment, it is in the moment that we stop that protecting and improving that real understanding can begin. Is that what you're saying?

TRUNGPA RINPOCHE: As far as this process is concerned, there's no promise of anything at all, none whatsoever. It's giving up everything, including the self.

S: Then that hopelessness puts you in the here and now.

TR: Much more than that. It doesn't put you anywhere. You have no ground to stand on, absolutely none. You are completely desolate. And even desolation is not regarded as home, because you are so desolately, absolutely hopeless that even loneliness is not a refuge any more. Everything is completely hopeless. Even *itself* [shouts "itself" and snaps fingers]. It's totally taken away from you, absolutely completely. Any kind of energy that's happening in order to preserve itself is also hopeless.

STUDENT: The energy that was preserving the self, that forms a kind of shell around the self, if that stops then it just escapes into no division between itself and what's all around it?

TRUNGPA RINPOCHE: It doesn't give you any reassurance. When we talk about hopelessness, it means literal hopelessness. The sense of hope here is hope as opposed to loss. There's no means by which you could get something in return any more at all. Absolutely not. Even itself.

S: It's lost its self?

TR: Lost itself, precisely.

S: That kind of groundlessness seems to be more than hopelessness. I mean, in hopelessness there's still some sense of there being *someone who* is without hope.

TR: Even that is suspicious.

S: What happens to the ground? The ground drops away. I don't understand.

TR: The ground is hopelessness as well. There's no solidity in the ground either.

S: I hear what you're saying. You're saying that no matter what direction one looks in—

TR: Yes, you are overwhelmed by hopelessness. All over. Utterly. Completely. Profusely. You are a claustrophobic situation of hopelessness.

We're talking about a sense of hopelessness as an *experience* of no ground. We are talking about experience. We are talking about an experience, which is one little thread in the whole thing. We are talking about the experience of hopelessness. This is an experience that cannot be forgotten or rejected. It might reject itself, but still there is experience. It is just a kind of thread that goes on. I thought we could discuss this further in connection with Padmasambhava's experience of experience. But the fact that this is Padmasambhava's experience of experience doesn't mean anything. It's still hopeless.

STUDENT: You seem to be saying that where there's no hope, it's intelligent. And when you think there's hope, then that's ignorance.

TRUNGPA RINPOCHE: I don't think so, my dear. It's completely hopeless.

STUDENT: When you talk about hopelessness, the whole thing seems totally depressing. And it seems you could very easily be overwhelmed by that depression to the point where you just retreat into a shell or insanity.

TRUNGPA RINPOCHE: It's up to you. It's completely up to you. That's the whole point.

S: Is there anything—

TR: You see, the whole point is that I'm not manufacturing an absolute model of hopelessness with complete and delicately worked-out patterns of all kinds, presenting it to you, and asking you to work on that. Your goodness, your hopelessness, is the only model there is. If I manufactured something, it would be just a trick, unrealistic. Rather, it's your hopelessness, it's your world, your family heirloom, your inheritance. That hopelessness comes in your existence, your psychology. It's a matter of bringing it out as it is. But it's still hopeless. As hopeful as you might try to make it, it's still hopeless. And I can't reshape it, remodel it, or refinish it at all. It's not like a political candidate going on television, where people powder his face and put lipstick on his mouth to make him presentable. One cannot do that. In this case it's hopeless; it's absolutely hopeless. You have to do it in your own way.

STUDENT: Is it possible for someone to be aware that it's all hopeless but yet be joyous?

TRUNGPA RINPOCHE: Well, I mean we could have all kinds of hopeless situations, but they are all the expression of hopelessness. I suppose what you described could happen, but who are you trying to con?

STUDENT: The situation with Naropa having his visions and having the possibility of choosing to jump over the bitch or deal with the bitch, is that the same situation of yes or no you described in your talk?

TRUNGPA RINPOCHE: I think so, yes.

S: And Naropa's hopelessness at the end—

TR: Naropa's state of hopelessness before he actually saw his guru was absolute. Understanding Padmasambhava's life without a sense of hopelessness would be completely impossible.

2

Hopelessness and the Trikaya

THE SENSE OF HOPELESSNESS is the starting point for relating with crazy wisdom. If the sense of hopelessness is able
to cut through unrealistic goals, then the hopelessness becomes something more definite. It becomes definite because
we are not trying to manufacture anything other than what
there is not. So a sense of hopelessness could provide the basic approach to nonduality.

The sense of hopelessness connects directly with the practical level of our everyday lives. Life on the practical level
does not contain any subtle philosophy or subtle mystical
experience. It just is. If we are able to see that isness, so to
speak, then there is a sense of realization. We experience
sudden enlightenment. Without a sense of hopelessness,
there is no way to give birth to sudden enlightenment. Only
giving up our projects brings about the ultimate, definite,
positive state of being, which is the realization that we are
already enlightened beings here and now.

In discussing the details of this state, we could say that
even in experiencing a sense of buddha-nature, we still have
to have that experience, which is connected with the samsaric, or confused, part of our being in that it is dependent

on the experience of something. Experience involves a sense of duality. You have an experience and you relate with that experience; you relate with it as something separate; there is a separation between you and what you experience. You are dealing with a subject matter, experience.

Though there is still a sense of separateness, of duality, nevertheless it is an experience of being awake, of realizing buddha within us. So we begin to develop some sense of space between the experience and the projection of the experience. There is a forward-moving journey of trying to catch some particular aspect in us that is sane. And making that effort, becoming involved in that particular relationship, brings our sense of space somewhere.

It is like when we are just about to say something. First we have to experience the unsaid things. We feel the space of what we haven't said yet. We feel the space, and then we say whatever we say, which accentuates the space in a certain way, makes it into a definite perspective. In order to express space, we have to draw the boundary of space.

That kind of sense of openness that happens when we are just about to say something or just about to experience something is a kind of sense of emptiness. It is a sense of fertile emptiness, pregnant emptiness. That experience of emptiness is the dharmakaya. In order to give birth, we have to have an accommodation for giving birth. The sense of the absence of that birth before giving birth is the dharmakaya.

Dharmakaya is unconditioned. The leap has already been made. When we definitely decide to leap, we have leapt already. The leaping itself is somewhat repetitious or redundant. Once we have already decided to leap, we have leapt. We are talking about that kind of sense of space in which the leap, the birth, is already given though not yet manifested. It is not yet manifested, but it is as good as already manifested. In that state of mind in which we are about to experience, say, drinking a cup of tea, we have drunk a cup of tea already before we drink it. And we have said things already before we actually say them on a manifest level.

That kind of pregnant, embryonic, fertile ground that happens in our state of mind constantly is also unconditioned [i.e., as well as pregnant with something]. It is unconditioned in relation to my ego, or dualistic mind, my actions, my love and hate, and so on. In relation to all that, it is unconditioned. Thus we have that kind of unconditioned glimpse happening in our state of mind constantly.

The dharmakaya state is the starting point or ground of Padmasambhava. The embryonic manifestation here is the *dharma*, the dharma of possibilities that have happened already, existing things that exist in nonexistence. It is the sense of fertility, complete fullness yet intangibility, in our daily experience. Before the emotions arise, there are preparations toward that. Before we put our actions into effect, there are preparations toward that. That sense of occupied space, self-existing space, is dharma. *Kaya* is form, or body, the statement that such dharma does exist. The body of dharma is the dharmakaya.

Then we have the second level of manifestation of Padmasambhava, the sambhogakaya, in our state of being. This is the borderline between fullness and emptiness. There is the sense that the fullness of it becomes valid, because it is emptiness. In other words, it is a kind of affirmation of the existence of emptiness. There is the spaciousness where the emotions begin to arise, where anger is just about to burst out or has burst out already, but there still needs to be a journey forward toward giving final birth. This [forward movement] is the sambhogakaya. *Sam* means "complete," *bhoga* means "joy." Joy here is occupation or energy, rather than joy in the sense of pleasure as opposed to pain. It is occupation, action existing for itself, emotions existing for themselves. But though they exist for themselves, they are rootless as far as basic validity is concerned. There is no basic validity, but still emotions occur out of nowhere, and their energy springs forth, sparks out, constantly.

Then we have nirmanakaya. *Nirmana* in this case is the emanation, or manifestation—the complete manifestation or final accent. It is like when a child has already been born and the doctor cuts the umbilical cord to make sure that the child is separate from its father and mother. It is now an independent entity. This is parallel to the bursting of the emotions into the fascinated world outside. At this point, the object of passion or the object of aggression, or whatever, comes out very powerfully and very definitely.

This does not particularly refer to applying the emotions; for example, using anger as an influence for killing a person or passion as an influence for magnetizing a person. Still, there is a sense that, before actual words are spoken or actual bodily movements have occurred, the emotions have occurred; there has been a final definition of the emotions and they have become separate from you. You have officially cut the umbilical cord between you and your emotions. They have already occurred outwardly—they have become a satellite already, your satellite already, a separate thing. This is final manifestation.

When we talk here about anger or passion or ignorance/bewilderment, whatever we talk about, we are not speaking in moralistic terms of good and bad. We are speaking of tremendously highly charged emotions that contain the energy of their vividness. We could say that our lives consist of this tremendous vividness all the time: the vividness of being bored, being angry, being in love, being proud, being jealous. Our lives consist of all these kinds of vividness rather than of virtues or sins created by those.

What we are talking about here is the essence of Padmasambhava. There is this vividness of Padmasambhava manifesting in our lives constantly through the process of giving birth: experiencing a sense of space, then manifesting, then finally concluding that manifestation. So there is the threefold process, of the dharmakaya as the embryonic space, the sambhogakaya as the forwarding quality, and the nirmanakaya in which it actually finally manifests itself. All those situations are the vividness of Padmasambhava.

It seems that before discussing the eight aspects of Padmasambhava, it is important to understand the three principles of the trikaya. Unless we realize the subtleties of the energies involved in Padmasambhava's life, we have no chance of understanding it. Without understanding the trikaya, we might think that when Padmasambhava manifests in the different aspects it is like one person wearing different hats: his business hat, his hunting hat, his yogi hat, his scholar hat, and so on. It is not like that. It is not like one person changing costumes; rather it has to do with the vividness of life.

In talking about Padmasambhava, we are not referring purely to a historical person: "once upon a time, there was a person Padmasambhava, who was born in India." Somehow that does not really make sense. If we were doing that, we would just be having a history lesson. Instead, what we are trying to point to here is that Padmasambhava is our experience. We are trying to relate with the Padmasambhava-*ness* in us, in our state of being. The Padmasambhava-ness consists of those three constituents: the dharmakaya, or open space; the sambhogakaya, or forward energy; and the nirmanakaya, or actual manifestation.

We might say to ourselves at this point: "This is supposed to be crazy wisdom; what's so crazy about those things? Energy happens, space is there; is there anything about this that is unusual, anything crazy or wise?" Actually there is nothing—nothing crazy about it and nothing wise about it. The only thing that makes it extraordinary is that it happens to be true. We are infested with Padmasambhava in ourselves. We are haunted by him. Our whole being is completely made out of Padmasambhava. So when we try to relate with him "out there," as a person who lives on a copper-colored mountain on some remote island off the coast of India, that does not make sense.

It would be very easy to relate with him that way, because then we could have a sense of ambition. We could feel that we would like to go where he is, or find out whether he is a purely mythical being or actually does exist. We could take a plane, we could take a boat; we could find out where those places are where Padmasambhava is still supposed to be living. Trying to invoke Padmasambhava, to bring him about in our being from the outside, is like waiting for Godot. The result never happens.

There was a great Tibetan siddha called the Madman of Tsang. He lived in Tsang, which is in East Tibet, near a mountain called Anye Machen, where my guru Jamgön Kongtrül visited him. This was about five years before I met my guru. He used to tell us the story of his meeting with the Madman of Tsang, who was an ordinary farmer who had achieved the essence of crazy wisdom. He had these very precious things stored in his treasury, bags and bags supposedly full of valuable things. But the bags turned out to contain just driftwood and rocks. My guru told us that he asked the Madman of Tsang, "How should we go about uniting ourselves with Padmasambhava?" The madman told him the following.

"When I was a young student and a very devout Buddhist, full of faith, I used to want my body to become one with Padmasambhava's body. I did countless recitations, thousands and millions of mantras and invocations. I used to shout myself half to death reciting mantras. I even felt that I was wasting my time by breathing in during these recitations. I called and called and called to Padmasambhava, trying to make my body one with his. But then suddenly I just realized: I *am*—my body *is*—Padmasambhava. I could go on calling on him until my voice breaks down, but it wouldn't make any sense. So I decided not to call on him any more. Then I found that Padmasambhava was calling on *me*. I tried to suppress it, but I couldn't control it. Padmasambhava wanted *me*, and he kept on calling *my* name."

This is the kind of situation we are discussing, I suppose. Instead of our looking out there for him, he is looking in at us. In order to make these things real and ordinary in our lives, it seems that we need some kind of conviction in us. We have to realize that there is a sense of energy that is always there, and that that energy contains totality. That energy is not dualistic or interdependent; it is a self-existing energy in us. We have our passion, our aggression; we have our own space, our own energy—it's there already. It exists without any dependency on situations. It is absolute and perfect and independent. It is free from any form of relationships.

That seems to be the point about Padmasambhava here. The principle of Padmasambhava consists in freedom from any speculative ideas or theories or activity of watching oneself. It is the living experience of emotions and experiences without a watcher. Because we are Buddha already, we are Padmasambhava already. Gaining such confidence, such vajra pride, gives us a further opportunity. It is not hard to imagine that when you know what you are and who you are completely, then you can explore the rest of the world, because you don't have to explore yourself any more.

STUDENT: Rinpoche, if the dharmakaya is a pregnant state already, or a fertile state already, does that mean that there isn't any completely empty dharmakaya that doesn't apply to anything? Are you saying that the dharmakaya always has some sense of application already?

TRUNGPA RINPOCHE: You see, the dharmakaya in this case is similar to experience. It's quite different from the *dharmadhatu,* the greater dharmadhatu. When you refer to it as *dharma* and *kaya,* it is, in some sense, conditioned. It's conditioned because it's pregnant already.[3]

S: So does that mean that the dharmadhatu is theoretical, purely a matter of theoretical background?

TR: I wouldn't even say it's theoretical. It hardly has a name at all. Talking about dharmadhatu makes us more self-conscious, so then dharmadhatu becomes self-conscious; or rather, inventing words about it makes dharmadhatu more self-conscious from our point of view.

S: Is dharmadhatu experientially different from dharmakaya?

TR: Yes. Dharmadhatu is no experience.

S: And that's the space in which the kayas—

TR: Take place, yes. Dharmakaya is already experience. Dharmakaya is referred to in Tibetan as *tangpo sangye,* which means "the primordial buddha," the buddha who never became a buddha through practice but who is realization on the spot. That is the nondualism of the dharmakaya. Whereas the dharmadhatu is total accommodation of some kind that doesn't have its own entity at all.

You see, the dharmakaya is, so to speak, a kind of credential. Somebody has to have a credential of some kind in order to be dharmakaya. That is why it is pregnant. But this sense of credential should not be regarded in a pejorative or negative way at all. The exciting things happening with the samsaric world are part of that manifestation. The dharma itself, as a teaching, is part of it; the teaching wouldn't exist unless there were somebody to teach. It's that kind of situation.

S: What does Padmasambhava have to do with the dharmadhatu?

TR: Nothing.

S: Well, what is the difference then between the sense of possibility in dharmakaya, the sense of a pregnant situation, and expectation in the negative buddhist sense of desire, of looking forward to something? In other words, you spoke of dharmakaya as a sense of possibility as if you had your tea before you even drank it. How does that differ from wanting a cup of tea in the grasping way?

TR: There's no difference at all. If we look at grasping in a matter-of-fact way, it's actually very spacious. But we regard grasping as an insult to ourselves. That's why it becomes an insult. But grasping as it is, is actually very spacious. It's a hollow question. Very spacious. That's the dharmakaya itself.

S: Is there a momentum that brings it beyond the sense of potential or pregnancy of the dharmakaya stage to the point where it is actually moving toward becoming something?

TR: There is momentum already, because there is experience. Momentum begins when you regard experience as something experience*able*. The momentum is there already, so dharmakaya is a part of that energy. That's why all three kayas are connected with energy. There is the most transparent energy, the energy of movement, and the energy of manifestation. Those three kayas are all included in that energy. That's why they are called kayas.

S: It seems as though within the pregnant space of the dharmakaya, there is also sambhogakaya and nirmanakaya.

TR: Yes.

S: It seems to me that in the journey from dharmakaya to nirmanakaya, if the manifestation is going to end up to be something samsaric and the dharmakaya is already pregnant with it, then there is a samsaric factor that is already part of the dharmakaya. For instance, if we have the cup of tea before we actually drink it, then there is all the conditioning from past tea-drinking experiences that are part of determining that experience.

TR: You see, the whole point when we talk about Padmasambhava is that Padmasambhava is the trikaya principle, which is made out of a combination of both samsara and nirvana at the same time, so any conditions or conditioning are valid. At this point, as far as that experience is concerned, samsara and nirvana are one within the experience. What we are concerned with here is that it is purely free energy. It's neither conditioned nor unconditioned, but rather its own existence is absolute in its own way. So we don't have to try to make it valid by persuading ourselves that there is nothing samsaric that is part of it. Without that [samsaric element], we would have nothing to be crazy about. This *is* crazy wisdom, you know.

S: What's the nirmanakaya part?

TR: The sense of relating with the tea as an external object, which is like cutting the umbilical cord. Relating with the tea as the teaness out there is the nirmanakaya. But this does not necessarily mean physically doing it, particularly. Rather it's that there are three types of solidification of experience related with tea, the threefold states of being of the mind.

S: So the nirmanakaya is the sort of "ness."

TR: Yes, it's the cupness and potness and teaness.

S: So what's the sambhogakaya?

TR: The sambhogakaya is the sense of slight separateness, as opposed to the abstract idea of having tea. There's some journey.

S: There's some sense in experiencing the potness and cupness that they might become exiled from the whole process of birth, cut off from the experiencing process that bore them in the first place?

TR: That's happened already. Once you are pregnant, it is already a statement of separation, and it is a further expression of separation when you give birth; then the final statement is when you cut the umbilical cord; that is the final state of separateness.

S: And you accept that separateness fully?

TR: Yes. Otherwise it becomes very confusing in terms of the partnership with nirvana, or whatever you would like to call it—sanity, nirvana.

STUDENT: I don't see how this relates with hopelessness. I mean, I don't see how these first two lectures go together.

TRUNGPA RINPOCHE: Well, hopelessness comes from the fact that this process we have been describing does not bring any comfort. We could say that dharmakaya exists, sambhogakaya exists, nirmanakaya exists, and each has its functions. But so what? Still there's no recipe for how to make yourself happy. At this point it has nothing to do with bringing happiness into our lives, or goodness or comfort or anything else like that. It's still a hopeless situation.

Realistically, even if you know the dharmakaya, sambhogakaya, and nirmanakaya from back to front, what does that mean to you? You will just understand the energy principle and the independence and potency of your energy. But apart from that, there's no medication. It's still hopeless.

STUDENT: Rinpoche, is seeing things as they are still experiential?

TRUNGPA RINPOCHE: Yes, we could say that seeing things as they are is not quite crazy enough.

STUDENT: Rinpoche, you've described the movement from dharmakaya to sambhogakaya to nirmanakaya as a movement of energy outward. Could that process be reversed? Does the energy also go from nirmanakaya to sambhogakaya to dharmakaya?

TRUNGPA RINPOCHE: That also happens constantly. It's sort of recycling itself. That's no big deal.

STUDENT: You've said that we have a choice between gradual and sudden realization.

TRUNGPA RINPOCHE: Yes.

S: Yet hopelessness is there all the time.

TR: Yes.

S: Well, what is it that we could do, then?

TR: There is an old saying that the path is the goal and the goal is the path. You make your journey, you get to your destination, and arriving at that destination brings on another question: how to proceed from there? In that way each goal itself becomes the path. Particularly from the tantric point of view, you don't achieve anything except path. Discovery of the path is achieving. You see what I mean?

S: Well, what's sudden about it?

TR: It's always sudden.

S: All the time.

TR: All the time, yes. Until you give up the path—and the goal—there's still sudden enlightenment all the time. So the only *final* sudden thing is that you have to give up sudden discovery. That's very shocking. And very sudden.

S: But that sudden flash that goes on all the time, you're saying, is different from the gradual path?

TR: Yes, definitely. The nature of the gradual path from this point of view, if I may say so, is that the gradual path regards the goal as the goal and the path as the doctrine. And the sudden path regards the path as the goal as well as the goal as the path. There's no room for doctrine. It is just a matter of personal experience all the time. If you had to give an Oxford dictionary definition of the difference between gradual and sudden enlightenment, that could be it.

STUDENT: Rinpoche, does this process of solidification from dharmakaya to nirmanakaya and the attitude toward it also apply on the psychological level to the process of projection—to your projections becoming more solid and your attitude toward that?

TRUNGPA RINPOCHE: Naturally. The whole existence of the three kayas is a kind projection in which you manufacture the projections. So in other words, the very existence of the dharma itself is a projection. Insanity or sanity both are projections. And since everything is done that way, the whole thing becomes a projection and solidity at the same time.

STUDENT: In the story of the man worshiping Padmasambhava with so many mantras and recitations, I wasn't sure of the point. Is that kind of devotional practice purely a waste of time? Or is there some value in it?

TRUNGPA RINPOCHE: Well, both are the same thing in a way. In order to gain valuation of time, to begin with you have to waste time, which is part of gaining valuation of time.

S: So he was wasting time?

TR: But he understood something out of it. He realized, finally, that he was wasting time, by wasting time.

S: Is that all that was happening there?

TR: Yes.

S: It doesn't sound like a waste of time at all.

TR: That's up to you. That's what I'm saying.

STUDENT: When you say the journey need never be made, do you really mean that? We don't have to make the trip?

TRUNGPA RINPOCHE: But then you don't know what the trip is.

S: Why do we need to know that?

TR: To realize you need never make it—it's a seamless web.

STUDENT: Is there a certain determinism involved in the dharmakaya? Is there a kind of inevitability in the progression from dharmakaya to sambhogakaya to nirmanakaya?

TRUNGPA RINPOCHE: I think probably the only determinism on the part of the dharmakaya is the self-consciousness of its own existence, of its own pregnancy. And that's the first expression of dualism.

STUDENT: What's the relation between the three kayas and the charnel ground you mentioned? Is there a relation?

TRUNGPA RINPOCHE: Each time you develop a manifestation, you create your own stuff—right at the beginning. Dharmakaya creates its own existence and its environment as well. The environment is the charnel ground—a place to dissolve, a place to manifest.

STUDENT: I don't see that strong a difference between the sambhogakaya and the nirmanakaya. The dharmakaya seems to have parent status, so to speak, and the sambhogakaya seems to be like giving birth—you know, first expression. And I don't see where the final step from the sambhogakaya to the nirmanakaya comes in. It seems that both of them represent completion of some sort.

TRUNGPA RINPOCHE: Well, the sambhogakaya is acknowledging the energy, you could say, and the nirmanakaya is executing, like the analogy of cutting the umbilical cord. Apart from that, there's no difference.

S: But the sambhogakaya, you said, was analogous to giving birth. That also seems pretty final.

TR: The sambhogakaya is acknowledging the energy in the sense of the receptiveness of reality. It is acknowledging that your projections are separate, definitely separate; and then what you do with the separateness, your projections, is handled by the nirmanakaya. The nirmanakaya could be described as the domestic matter of how to handle your kitchen-sink problem, whereas the sambhogakaya is like getting married to begin with to create the kitchen-sink problem. And the dharmakaya is like courting; it contains those possibilities, is already fraught with all kinds of possibilities.

S: Before, I thought you said that this process of the trikaya, looked at in the context of the self, would be samsaric, whereas in the context of the dharmadhatu, it would be nirvanic?

TR: We never discussed the nirvana aspect of it, because for one thing it becomes too idealistic. For another thing it becomes inaccurate, because we never see it. So we are speaking from the samsaric point of view of enlightenment at this point.

S: Why don't we see it?

TR: We still want to have answers and conclusions, which is an experience of separateness, which is samsaric. You want logic, and logic depends on samsaric mind.

S: It seems that this three-kaya process is a different perspective on the same process as the twelve nidanas and the six realms of the world and the different pardo states. Is that so?

TR: Same thing.

3

Fearlessness

HAVING ALREADY DISCUSSED the three-kaya principle by
way of preparation, we might now consider Padmasambhava
as a representative of crazy wisdom as opposed to any other
type of manifestation of a vidyadhara. We might say that the
unique quality of crazy wisdom in Padmasambhava's case is
that of sudden enlightenment. The eight aspects of Padmasambhava are not a lineal process, they are simultaneous. In
fact, the traditional expression is "eight names" of Padmasambhava rather than "eight aspects."

What is the name principle? Why is it called a *name*
rather than *aspect?* When we refer to aspects, usually we are
referring to differences in basic being. We might speak of a
man's father aspect, his teacher aspect, his businessman aspect. In this ordinary usage, there is the idea of a change
that goes with the different roles. This usual idea of different aspects—which would imply that Padmasambhava transformed himself, entered into different parts of his being, or
manifested different expressions—does not apply to Padmasambhava. Rather, his having different names is connected
with the attitudes of his students and of other beings toward
him. The different names have to do with the different ways

other people see Padmasambhava rather than with his changing. So *name* here has the sense of *title*. The Tibetan phrase is *guru tsen gye,* "the eight names of the guru." *Tsen* is the honorific Tibetan word for "name." Some people might see Padmasambhava as fatherly, others as brotherly, and still others might see him as an enemy. The views imposed by the way people see him are the basis for the eight names of Padmasambhava. Nevertheless, his only manifestation is that of crazy wisdom.

A description for a crazy-wisdom person found in the scriptures is: "He subdues whoever needs to be subdued and destroys whoever needs to be destroyed." The idea here is that whatever your neurosis demands, when you relate with a crazy-wisdom person you get hit back with that. Crazy wisdom presents you with a mirror reflection. That is why Padmasambhava's crazy wisdom is universal. Crazy wisdom knows no limitation and no logic regarding the form it takes. A mirror will not compromise with you if you are ugly. And there is no point in blaming the mirror or breaking it. The more you break the mirror the more reflections of your face come about from further pieces of the mirror. So the nature of Padmasambhava's wisdom is that it knows no limitation and no compromise.

The first aspect of Padmasambhava is called Pema Gyalpo or, in Sanskrit, Padma Raja. Padma Raja was born in the Himalayan region between India and Afghanistan, in a place called Uddiyana that has since been called Swat. It was a very beautiful place surrounded by snow-capped mountains. The whole area resembled a man-made park. There were lakes and lotus ponds; the air was fresh, the climate ideal. One of the lakes was called Dhanakosha, or also, Lake Sindhu. It was covered with the leaves and petals of lotuses. One particular lotus was unusually huge and did not follow the usual pattern of changing with the seasons. It appeared at the beginning of the Year of the Monkey and continued its growth straight through the seasons. Winter came, spring came, autumn came, and summer came, and the lotus never opened. At last, on the tenth day of the tenth month of the Year of the Monkey, the lotus opened. There was a beautiful child inside, sitting on the calyx of the lotus. He had the appearance of a child of eight. He was dignified and inquisitive. The bees and birds congregated about this beautiful child, praising him. The sound of music without a player was heard. The whole place was pervaded with a sense of wholesomeness, health, and mystery.

The child looked like a well-looked-after prince. Could that be possible? He had no fear and seemed to be amused by his surroundings, constantly fascinated by the world outside.

That was the birth of Padmasambhava.

The whole point here is the infant quality of Padmasambhava. He was an aged infant—this is a contradiction, of course—a beautiful grown-up infant, an infant who was wise and powerful, an infant who did not nurse on milk or eat any other food, but who lived on thin air. It is because of this youthfulness that he is known as Padma Raja, "Prince of the Lotus."

We have that element of youthfulness in us as well. We have that beautiful infantlike quality in us. The experience that has taken place in our life situation is like the mud surrounding the roots of a lotus at the bottom of a lake. There is desire, passion, aggression, neurosis of all kinds. Nevertheless, out of these, some quality of freshness comes up always: that infant quality in us, completely young, youthful, inquisitive, comes up.

The inquisitiveness of that infant aspect in us is not neurotically inquisitive, but basically inquisitive. Since we want to explore the depth of pain, since we want to explore the warmth of joy, doing so seems natural. This is the Padma-sambhava quality in us. We could call it buddha-nature or basic enlightenment. We would like to pick up a toy, hold it in our hands, explore it, drop it, bash it around, see it falling apart, unscrew it, put it together. We always do that, just as an infant does. This infant quality is the quality of enlightenment.

When people talk about enlightenment, they usually have the idea of someone old and wise. An enlightened person, they think, is one who has been aged by experience and has thus become wise; in fact, learned. He has collected hundreds of millions of pieces of information. This makes him old and wise, trustworthy and good—enlightened. But from the point of view of crazy wisdom, enlightenment is entirely different from this. It doesn't particularly have anything to do with being old and wise. It is more like being young and wise, because it has tremendous openness toward exploring the experiences that go on in our lives—toward exploring them psychologically, on the relationship level, on the domestic level, on the practical level, on the philosophical level, and so forth.

There is also a quality of fearlessness in enlightenment, not regarding the world as an enemy, not feeling that the world is going to attack us if we do not take care of ourselves. Instead, there is tremendous delight in exploring the razor's edge, like a child who happens to pick up a razor blade with honey on it. It starts to lick it; it encounters the sweet taste and the blood dripping off its tongue at the same time. Simultaneous pain and pleasure are worth exploring, from the point of view of the sanity of crazy wisdom. This [natural inquisitiveness] is the youthful-prince quality of Padmasambhava. It is the epitome of noncaring but at the same time caring so very much—being eager to learn and eager to explore.

Probably the word *learn* is wrong here. It is not learning in the sense of collecting information; rather, it is absorbing what is happening around us, constantly relating to it. In this kind of learning, we do not at all learn things so that we can use them at some point to defend ourselves. We learn things because they are pleasurable to learn, fantastic to learn. It is like children playing with toys. They discover toys out of nowhere: they are not educational toys, but just things that are around.

Padmasambhava was born from a lotus without parents, because he had no need to be educated. He had no need for parents to bring him up to responsible, sensible adulthood. It is said that he was born from a lotus as though already eight years old. But we could say he was born from a lotus as though already eighty years old. There's no age limit. Whatever his age, he would still be a young baby, or let's say an old baby. Both amount to the same thing.

One of the most important points here is a sense of exploration of our state of being that is independent of education and information-collecting. We just explore because we are delighted, like children playing with toys. That childlike quality is always in us, constantly. That is the quality of Padmasambhava.

Once again, this quality also contains fearlessness. The problem we have with fearlessness is that our samsaric way of approaching things prevents us from exploring freely. Although we have a tremendous yearning toward it, we feel that we might get hurt if we explore too much. That is fear. The infant quality of Padmasambhava is fearless, because he is not concerned with being hurt. It is not that he is masochistic or sadistic at all. It is just that he has a sense of appreciation, a sense of complete openness in relating with things—simply, directly. He does not relate with things because they are educational, but just because they are there. The relationship just happens, it develops.

The young prince born from a lotus was discovered by Indrabhuti, the king of Uddiyana. For a long time, King Indrabhuti had been praying to be granted a son, but he had been unable to have one. One day one of his court attendants went to Lake Dhanakosha to collect flowers for the royal household and discovered the mysterious lotus. It had opened, and a young and funny, inquisitive and beautiful child was sitting on it. The attendant reported this to the king, who decided to have the child brought back to the court and to adopt him as his son, as the future king.

Padmasambhava explored the pleasurable situations in the royal palace. After sometime food and wealth and comforts of all kinds began to bore him. Indrabhuti decided to arrange a marriage for Padmasambhava with the daughter of a neighboring king so that Padmasambhava would have a playmate. The marriage took place and Padmasambhava continued to explore things. He explored sexuality, companionship, food, wealth, and so on.

One thing I would like to make completely clear here is that this whole situation was not just a matter of Padmasambhava having to grow up or gain information about life. Padmasambhava's becoming a prince—even the very fact of his being born in a lotus—was not his trip, so to speak, but Indrabhuti's trip. Indrabhuti's version of Padmasambhava had to be given food and clothes and the companionship of women. Padmasambhava then broke through that hospitality by dancing on the palace roof holding a trident and a vajra. He was dancing around up there, and as if by accident, he let go of his two scepters and they fell from the roof. The trident pierced the heart of a minister's wife who was walking below, and the vajra landed on her son's skull. Both mother and child died instantly.

What do you think happened next? Padmasambhava was expelled from the kingdom. His deed was against the law. Murderers were not allowed in the kingdom. Everything in the kingdom was done properly, in accordance with law, so even that mysterious child born from a lotus had to leave— which is what Padmasambhava was asking for. He was going to cut through that situation and continue his explorations of all kinds.

Of course, we as students do not necessarily have to follow Padmasambhava's style exactly. We do not necessarily have to go through all the processes that he went through. In fact it would be impossible; our situation would not permit it. Nevertheless, his example of exploring passion and aggression is a very, very interesting one—one worth relating to, worth exploring. However, being able to explore depends on fearlessness. Our degree of fearlessness should be, so to speak, the speedometer of our sanity [i.e., the indicator of how far we can go]. The awakened state of mind is shining through [and to the extent that it is, we go ahead]. As the scriptures say, an ordinary person should not act like a yogi, a yogi should not act like a bodhisattva, a bodhisattva should not act like a siddha, and a siddha should not act like a buddha. If we go beyond our limit, if we decide to get wild and freak out, we get hurt. We get feedback: a very strong message comes back to us. If we go beyond our limit, it becomes destructive.

So the idea of crazy wisdom is not just getting wild and freaking out. Rather, it is relating with your fear. How much you explore depends on how much fundamental fear has been related with—I wouldn't say conquered. If you do it in accordance with how much fundamental fear you have related with, then you are not going beyond your limitation.

So, strangely enough, it could be said that crazy wisdom

is very timid or cowardly. Cowardice breeds crazy wisdom. Discretion is the better part of valor.

Crazy wisdom is unlike any of the other notions of the path we have discussed elsewhere. For example, in the bodhisattva path you age or grow up from the first bhumi to the second and so on up to the tenth, and then, finally, the eleventh, the enlightened state. The teaching concerning the bodhisattva path is based on aging, growing old, gaining more and more experience. You collect one paramita after the other. You gain information, understanding, and by building yourself up higher and higher, you become a great scholar as well as a great buddha in some sense. But as far as Padmasambhava's example is concerned, there is no notion of enlightment and realization coming about through collecting stuff, experiences. Padmasambhava's style is one of purely experiencing life situations as a spontaneously existing infant, and being willing to be an infant forever. One of the terms developed in the maha ati tradition for this principle is *shönü pum ku,* "youthful prince in a vase."

The vase represents an embryonic situation—embryonic but at the same time youthful. Breaking the vase is reversing the trikaya principle. You have gained dharmakaya; when the vase is broken, you come back down to sambhogakaya and nirmanakaya; you come back down to earth. A similar process is symbolized by the Zen oxherding pictures. After the point where there is no more ox and no more oxherd, you return to the world.

So the main focus here is the youthfulness of the enlightened state of being. This youthfulness is the immediacy of experience, the exploratory quality of it.

"But wouldn't exploring age us, make us old?" we might ask. We have to put so much energy into exploring. Do we not become like a traveler who grows old through traveling? From the point of view of crazy wisdom, this is not the case.

Exploring is no strain. You might have to do the same thing again and again, but each time you discover new facets of it, which makes you younger.

Discovery is related with energy that feeds you constantly. It brings your life to a very full, healthy state. So each time you explore, you gain new health. You constantly come back to a sense of being up to date in your experience of the world, of your life. So the whole thing becomes constant rejuvenation.

Now that the Padma Raja, the beautiful child, has been kicked out of his kingdom and is wandering somewhere in the suburbs of Indrabhuti's city, experiencing charnel grounds and wastelands with their poisonous snakes, tigers, and so on, let us pause in our story.

STUDENT: The "prince in the vase" already has the dharmakaya quality. When you break the vase, that begins his movement back toward nirmanakaya?

TRUNGPA RINPOCHE: Yes. It is reversing the trikaya.

S: Padmasambhava was born already dharmakayalike?

TR: Yes. Then he comes down to earth. The gravity pull is compassion. Once you are dharmakaya, you can't just stay there. You return to the world by means of the sambhogakaya and the nirmanakaya.

STUDENT: I encountered the metaphor you used of licking honey from a razor blade in *The Life and Teaching of Naropa*.[4] There it appeared as a simile connected with the Four Noble Truths, that is, portraying suffering that ought to be avoided or that an enlightened person would avoid, knowing it was there. Does your use of it here mean that from Padmasambhava's viewpoint the Four Noble Truths are no longer true?

TRUNGPA RINPOCHE: It's a different way of approaching the Truths—or not exactly different, but authentic, we might say. Here suffering is not regarded as something that you should avoid or abandon; rather, it should be regarded as truth. See what I mean?

S: It's what you taste.

TR: It's what you taste, yes, while exploring the subtleties of everything as an infant would.

S: Does that exploration have to be painful?

TR: Pain is arbitrary at this point. Experiences are not particularly regarded as painful or pleasurable. They just are.

STUDENT: You said that the child was fearless. And then you said that cowardice is the path. Aren't those two contradictory?

TRUNGPA RINPOCHE: They both amount to the same thing at this point. You are fearless because you don't go beyond certain limitations; you are fearless "as it is," and therefore you are a coward at the same time. That may be very difficult to grasp. I don't know whether I am making myself clear.

STUDENT: I have the same question. When you tell us, "It's up to you," it seems that we have a choice about what our limitations are, almost as though we created them ourselves.

TRUNGPA RINPOCHE: I don't see why not, because your limitations are *your* limitations.

S: They don't feel like *my* limitations. They're something that I discover as I go along.

TR: Well, you had to discover them, so you manufactured them as you went along.

S: You mean to say, if I wanted to, I could discover other limitations instead?

TR: Precisely! That's the whole point.

S: What's the point about going beyond them? You seemed to say that crazy wisdom discouraged going beyond them.

TR: Yes.

S: Going beyond them would be like going into some realm of utter fear or something?

TR: Well, this is very simple—kindergarten level. Going beyond your limitations is making things up rather than actually going beyond your limitations. It's manufacturing a dream world.

S: Are you making a distinction between made-up limitations and more real ones?

TR: Sure.

S: And you shouldn't try to go beyond the more real ones?

TR: You can't go beyond them anyway. They're real ones. You can't. You can't relate with them. You'd be going beyond your strength.

S: Then there's no danger of going beyond the natural limitation?

TR: Well, one tends very often to try to explore it.

S: Then what's the difference between exploring it and going beyond it?

TR: The difference is, if you go beyond your own limitation you get hurt. You get some message.

S: So how does fearlessness apply in this situation?

TR: You see, the point is, we do not even trust our own

abilities. Usually we don't. That's where fearlessness could play an important part—in exploring the complete realm of your strength. But then going beyond that is frivolous; if you do that you're subject to destruction. So fearlessness is not a matter of doing something outrageous outside of your realm, but of exploring the complete range of your whole strength.

S: What would keep a fearless person from exploring beyond his own strength?

TR: Some message will come back to that person.

S: Would that really prevent a person who is fearless from going beyond, from exploring everything?

TR: Fearlessness is still a conditional situation; such a person wouldn't be fearless of *everything*.

S: Is this the use of cowardice as intelligence?

TR: Yes.

S: Is that the wisdom part of crazy wisdom?

TR: Somewhat. If you regard crazy wisdom as just being completely outrageous, that's not particularly good or healthy. You are letting yourself in for destruction. That's the usual idea people have, you know: if you're trying to freak out, just push more, push more.

S: It seems that such boundaries presuppose a structure that is independent of oneself—a structure of boundaries out there beyond which a person shouldn't really venture.

TR: Not quite. It is dependent upon one's relationship with the structure.

S: The message that I get out of all this is, one should try to be aware of one's limitations so as not to step over them and get hurt.

TR: Not exactly. It's a question of being cautious.

S: How do you know when you're being cautious? This seems to be the point. How do you know when you should pull back or when you should go forward?

TR: You have to relate to what's happening in the whole process. When you begin to notice a deceptive attitude like "Maybe I could try something better than this," then you have begun to develop fear already because you haven't actually ventured into that area before. A warning comes from the sense of self-deception.

S: How do you become aware of that deception?

TR: It's very obvious. Only we know ourselves. We are the closest person to ourselves that we have. We know when we are deceiving ourselves and when we are not. There's no demonstration needed for that. That's something that's understood between you and yourself.

S: Probably a teacher is very helpful to encourage you in certain areas.

TR: You have your areas already. You already have the possibility of rediscovering your strengths and abilities. Teachers can't follow you, live with you, be your bedfellows all the time. Your teacher cannot always be there to guide you, but your self-deception guides you all the time.

STUDENT: Does karma begin to form in the dharmakaya?

TRUNGPA RINPOCHE: We run into different philosophical opinions of different schools on this point. Some people say that no karma develops at that point, and some say that there is karma in the dharmakaya, because the dharmakaya is also a separate entity and has an allegiance toward nirvana. Longchen Rabjam, the great maha ati teacher, would say that karma has developed already; so our school would say that karma has developed already at the dharmakaya level. The dharmakaya brings you a message of sanity because of the insanity that you have already. So that is a relational action; relational action has already happened. In other words, the potter's wheel of the second nidana has already developed.

STUDENT: Why does Padmasambhava choose such a dramatic means of expressing his dissatisfaction with living in a palace? Why does he have to throw a trident and drop his vajra, piercing a heart and cracking a skull? Why doesn't he just walk out?

TRUNGPA RINPOCHE: Walking out sounds like a cop-out. For him just to disappear and just be discovered as missing sounds like the action of a very transparent person who's afraid to communicate with anything and just flees. Padmasambhava is much more heavy-handed than that.

STUDENT: Is fear something other than just projections?

TRUNGPA RINPOCHE: Fear is the message as well as the radar. It is usually a relationship situation. It's not absolute. It's not independent of dualism. I think the crazy-wisdom approach to fear is not regarding it as a hangup alone, but realizing it is intelligent. It has a message of its own. Fear is worth respecting. If we dismiss fear as an obstacle and ignore it, then we might end up with accidents. In other words, fear is a very wise message.

S: My experience of fear is that it seems to be a really major manifestation of my confusion. One of the daily experiences is that it's a lie and a trap, a tremendous energy trap. I just try to keep from getting caught up in the impulse of it.

TR: Well you see, the point is, you can't con fear or

frighten fear. You have to respect fear. You might try to tell yourself that it's not real, that it's just false. But that kind of approach is very questionable. It is better to develop some kind of respect, realizing that neurosis also is a message, rather than garbage that you should just throw away. That's the whole starting point—the idea of samsara and nirvana being one. Samsara is not regarded as a nuisance alone, but it has its own potent message that is worthy of respect.

S: I'm far from throwing it away, but at the same time, I don't want to centralize it as an issue, to make a mystery out of it. So it's a very fine balance between not throwing it away and trying to let it go.

TR: Well, you have experience already and you don't have to question the experiencer on how to handle it diplomatically.

S: There doesn't seem to be much choice. The fear has such tremendous power.

TR: Well, that's fine. Then you have no chance to think about it or strategize it. Just leap.

S: There's a kind of fear that's a threat to the ego, when it's one of your illusions that feels threatened. Is there a difference between that kind of fear and the fear of going beyond your real limitations?

TR: There seems to be one, yes. There is the fear of not being able to handle what you have, and there's also a sense of needing something more than what you have. Hesitation to deal with what you have can be conquered by a leap, but needing to improvise further entertainment is a deception.

S: The deception of going beyond your limitations.

TR: Yes.

S: Can you take a leap without worrying about your limitations?

TR: Well, if you can, leap. Otherwise, you can't leap either. If you can, take a leap. Then, as you leap, you come back naturally [to the proper relationship to your limitations]. Unless you try to take a sensational leap. In that case, you don't even know what you're doing, but you do it because you want to entertain yourself. It's like taking an overdose.

STUDENT: Is the sense of discovery you talk about the same as keeping your space open, or is it a different idea?

TRUNGPA RINPOCHE: Well, that seems to be it. Discovery doesn't have to be a manifestation of something. It's an attitude of being willing to accommodate whatever comes along. It is somewhat a sense of the duality of something.

S: Quite often in spiritual trips, particularly when they have spectacular practices, there's a tendency to want some practice that you don't know anything about. Would you think of that as a case of helpful inquisitiveness or discovery?

TR: Not if you don't know what you're getting into. There's a difference between exploring what is there and exploring what isn't there. When a child is playing with the razor's edge, the razor is there and the honey is there on the razor's edge. But if the child is exploring something outside, beyond the edge of the balcony, there's nothing beyond the balcony except a sheer drop. That is suicidal.

STUDENT: When one comes to crazy wisdom, why does one man become like the Madman of Tsang and another become a person like your guru?

TRUNGPA RINPOCHE: I think it just depends on our manifestation and our way of viewing things. It's a question of what we are ready for. My guru was the audience for the

Madman of Tsang, and I was the audience for my guru. I wasn't all that crazy at the time, so he wasn't very crazy. But the Madman of Tsang was as crazy as he was because my guru was crazy enough to relate with it.

Nyima Öser

4

Death and the Sense of Experience

THE YOUTHFUL PRINCE'S EXPLORATION of life situations is connected with a sense of eternity. Exploring life situations is making friends with the world, and making friends with the world consists of regarding the world as trustworthy. [It becomes trustworthy because] there is something eternal about it. When we talk about eternity, we are not talking about the eternity of one particular entity continuing on and on, as in the philosophical beliefs of the eternalists. In this case discontinuity is also an expression of eternity. But before discussing eternity, it might be good to discuss death.

Death is the desolate experience in which our habitual patterns cannot continue as we would like them to. Our habitual patterns cease to function. A new force, a new energy, takes us over, which is "deathness," or discontinuity. It is impossible to approach that discontinuity from any angle. That discontinuity is something you cannot communicate with, because you cannot please that particular force. You can't make friends with it, you can't con it, you can't talk it into anything. It is extremely powerful and uncompromising.

This uncompromisingness also blocks expectations for the future. We have our plans—projects of all kinds that we would like to work on. Even if we are bored with life, we would still like to be able to recover that boredom. There is constant hope that something better might come out of the painful situations of life, or that we might discover some further way to expand pleasurable situations. But the sense of death is very powerful, very organic, and very real.

When you are about to die, it may be that your doctors, your relatives, or your closest friends won't tell you you are going to die. They might find it difficult to communicate this to you. But they communicate an unspoken sympathy, and there is something behind it.

In the conventional world, people do not want to relate with a friend who is dying. They do not want to relate to their friend's experience of death as something personal. It is a mutual embarrassment, a mutual tragedy that they don't want to talk about. If we belong to less conventional circles, we might approach a dying person and say, "You are dying," but at the same time we try to tell him: "After all, this is nothing bad that's happening to you. You are going to be okay. Think of those promises about ongoing eternity you've heard. Think of God, think of salvation." We still don't want to get to the heart of the matter. We don't talk about purgatory or hell or the tormenting experience of the pardo. We are trying to face the situation, but it is embarrassing. Though we are brave enough to say that someone is going to die, we say: "But still, you're going to be okay. Everybody around you feels positive about this, and we love you. Take the love that we feel toward you with you and make something of it as you pass from this world, as you die." That's the attitude [of avoidance] we have toward death.

The actual experience of death, as I have already explained, is a sense of ceasing to exist. The normal routine of your daily life ceases to function and you turn into something else. The basic impact of the experience is the same whether you believe in rebirth or not: it is the discontinuity of what you are doing. You are leaving your present associates behind. You will no longer be able to read that book that you didn't finish. You will not be able to continue the course you were taking. Maybe people who are involved with the doctrine of rebirth might try to tell you, "When you come back, you will finish this book. You'll be back with us. Maybe you'll be one of our children. Think of those possibilities." They tend to say those kinds of things and make promises of all kinds. They make promises about being with God or coming back to the world and continuing with things you have left behind.

In this kind of talk, there is something that is not quite open. There is some kind of fear, mutual fear, even in spite of beliefs about eternity or reincarnation. There is fear or embarrassment about relating to death. There is always a feeling of something undesirable, even if you are reading your friend a chapter from *The Tibetan Book of the Dead*,[5] or whatever. You might tell your friend, "Though something terrible is happening to you, there is a greater thing. Now you are actually going to have a chance to get into those experiences described in *The Tibetan Book of the Dead*. And we'll help you do it!" But no matter what we try, there is this sense of something that can't be made all right, no matter what kind of positive picture we try to paint.

It seems, quite surprisingly, that for many people, particularly in the West, reading *The Tibetan Book of the Dead* for the first time is very exciting. Pondering on this fact, I have come to the conclusion that the excitement comes from the fact that tremendous promises are being made. Fascination with the promises made in the *Book of the Dead* almost undermines death itself. We have been looking for so long for a way to undermine our irritations, including death itself. Rich people spend a lot of money on coffins, on makeup for the corpse, on good clothes to dress it up in. They pay for expensive funeral systems. They will try any way at all to undermine the embarrassment connected with death. That is why *The Tibetan Book of the Dead* is so popular and is considered to be so fantastic.

People were very excited and celebratory about the idea of reincarnation in the same way. A few decades ago when the idea of reincarnation became current for the first time, everybody was excited about it. That's another way of undermining death. "You're going to continue; you have your karmic debts to work out and your friends to come back to. Maybe you will come back as my child." Nobody stopped to consider that they might come back as a mosquito or a pet dog or cat.

The type of approach to death we have been discussing is very strange, extremely strange.

When we discuss the discovery of eternity by Vajradhara, as the next aspect of Padmasambhava is called, we are not looking at it as a victory over death or as a replacement for the irritations of death or anything of that nature. Eternity in this sense is connected with a true vision of the facts of life. Pain exists and pleasure exists. A negative aspect of the world does exist. Yet you can still relate with it. Fundamentally, developing this kind of sense of eternity is making friends. We might regard a certain person as a good friend in spite of his threatening qualities. In fact, that is the reason we become friends.

Relating with eternity in this sense is becoming a king of life, a lord of life. And if the lord of life is really a lord, his empire extends to death as well. So the lord of life is the lord of life and death. And this lord of life is known as Vajradhara.

The young prince who has just fled from his kingdom suddenly decides to adapt to the savagery of the charnel ground and to the fundamental principle of eternity, which is often known as the mahamudra experience. The mahamudra experience here is the experience that relates with the living quality of phenomena. That is to say, the whole scene in the charnel ground is *real*. There are skeletons, pieces of bodies, wild animals, ravens, jackals, and so forth.

In the charnel ground, the young prince discovers a new approach to life, or rather, a new approach to life discovers him. We could say that at this stage Padmasambhava becomes a solid citizen, because the sense of eternity brings indestructibility, indestructibility in the sense that nothing can be a threat and nothing can produce comfort. That is the kind of eternity we are referring to here. Death is no longer regarded as a threat. Padmasambhava's experience of death is an experience of one of the aspects of life. He is not concerned with perpetuating his personality and existence. We could say that this approach is more than the yogi's or siddha's approach. This approach is more that of a buddha, since these experiences are not regarded as achievements of any kind—they are not discoveries, victories, or forms of revenge. These experiences simply take place; and because they happen, Padmasambhava tunes in to them. So Padmasambhava as Vajradhara becomes the lord of life and death, the holder of the vajra, the holder of indestructible energy—a sambhogakaya buddha.

The next journey that Padmasambhava makes is connected with his wanting to explore all kinds of teaching situations and wanting to relate with the great teachers of the world of that time. He visits one of the leading teachers of the maha ati tradition, Shri Simha, who supposedly came from Thailand, Siam, and was living in a cave in another charnel ground. Vajradhara, the sambhogakaya aspect of Padmasambhava, went and asked him how to destroy the sense of experience. And Shri Simha reduced Padmasambhava to the syllable HUM, which is penetration. You don't try to dissolve experience or try to regard it as a fallacy. You penetrate experience. Experience is like a container with lots of holes in it, which means that it cannot give you proper shelter, proper comfort. Penetrating or puncturing this is like puncturing a comfortable hammock hanging underneath a tree: [once it is punctured,] when you approach it and try to sit in it, you find that you end up on the ground. That's the penetration of the seed syllable HUM. Reducing Padmasambhava to HUM, Shri Simha swallows him through his mouth and shits him out through his anus. This is bringing him to the nirmanakaya experience of being able to penetrate the phenomenal world thoroughly and completely, of being able to transmit a message to the phenomenal world.

Having destroyed his own sense of survival and achieved a sense of eternity, Padmasambhava now develops a sense of penetration. (Of course, he isn't really developing anything, he is just going through these phases. We are telling the story of Padmasambhava in accordance with how we have manufactured him, rather than trying to express that he did all those things.) This is when Padmasambhava became known as the great yogi who could control time, who could control day and night and the four seasons. This yogi aspect of Padmasambhava is called Nyima Öser. Nyima Öser penetrated all the conceptualizations of time, day and night, the four seasons. In his iconography, he is seen holding the sun still, using its rays as a tether.

The idea here is not that some achievement of a subtle experience can bring you to such complete absorption that you cease to experience the distinctions between night and day and the four seasons. Rather, the conceptualized attitudes toward day and night and the four seasons—or toward pain and pleasure or whatever—are penetrated through. Usually day and night and the four seasons bring us comfort by giving us the feeling we are relating with reality, with the elements: "Now we are relating with summer, now we are relating with autumn, now we are relating with winter, and now we are relating with spring. How good to be alive! How good to be on earth, man's best place, his home! It's getting late; it's time for dinner. We could begin the day with a hearty breakfast." And so forth. Our life-style is governed by these concepts. There are lots of things to do as time goes along, and relating with them is like swinging in a hammock, a comfortable bed in the open air. But Nyima Öser punctured this hammock. Now you can't have a good time swinging and having a comfortable snooze in the open air. That's the penetrating quality here.

STUDENT: You are having a comfortable snooze in this hammock. Then you penetrate the comfortable appearance of this hammock. So where does that leave you—standing up?

TRUNGPA RINPOCHE: You find yourself on the ground.

S: But alert somehow?

TR: Yes. One of the qualities seems to be a sense of awake rather than absorption.

STUDENT: If Padmasambhava is the great yogi who controls time, does that mean that time doesn't control him the way it does us?

TRUNGPA RINPOCHE: It's not really a matter of controlling time; or not being controlled by it. It's discovering timelessness. If you translate this into a kind of peasant language, then you could say "controlling time."

STUDENT: You have repeatedly emphasized that Padmasambhava doesn't learn anything and in a sense knows everything. I don't understand why we can't look upon him as an ordinary human, like any one of us, who has learned various things at various stages.

TRUNGPA RINPOCHE: We could equally well relate with our own stages in this way. Our process of spiritual development, or whatever you want to call it, is an unlearning process rather than one of collecting new experiences. Padmasambhava's style is unmasking, unlearning—layers and layers of phenomenal covering are gradually removed.

S: The unmasking, or unlearning, process seems to be like a series of deaths. Why does that have to be so painful? Why can't it be like a kind of liberation and have a kind of joyous feeling?

TR: Well, it is joyous, and maybe we are complaining too much. We are more aware of the intensity of the darkness than of the brilliance of the light.

S: It seems that the proper way to relate to death is without any strategy. Do you have to give up your fear before you can be without a strategy? Or can you just relate to your fear?

TR: Fear is a very interesting thing, actually. It has insight as well as the panicky blind quality. So it seems that if you give up hope of attaining anything, then tuning in to fear is tuning in to insight. And skillful means arises spontaneously out of fear itself, because fear seems to be extremely resourceful. It is the opposite of hopelessness, in fact. But fear also has the element of panic and the deaf and dumb quality—you know, doing the best you can. But fear without hope seems to be something very insightful.

S: Is fear insightful in that it points to why you were afraid in the first place?

TR: Not only that. It has its own intuitive aspect going

beyond just logical conclusions. It has spontaneously existing resourcefulness.

S: Could you say more about that?

TR: When you connect with your fear, you realize you have already leapt, you are already in mid-air. You realize that, and then you become resourceful.

S: Isn't that what we are all doing—being resourceful out of nowhere?

TR: We don't realize that we're already in mid-air.

STUDENT: Rinpoche, you say that fear without hope would be intelligent. Could the same be said about the other intense emotions?

TRUNGPA RINPOCHE: Hope and fear largely constitute the rest of the emotions. Hope and fear represent the kind of pushing and pulling quality of duality, and all the emotions consist of that. They are different aspects of that; they all seem to be made out of hope and fear of something—pulling and magnetizing or fending off.

S: Is having fear also desire of the same thing you are afraid of?

TR: Yes, that's the way it is. But when you realize that there is nothing to be desirous *of* (you know, the desire is the hope aspect of the fear), when you realize that, then you and your fear are left nakedly standing alone.

S: So you just connect with the fear without hope. But how do you do that?

TR: It's relating without feedback. Then the situation automatically intensifies or becomes clear.

S: Can you apply the same approach to anger? If I'm angry, instead of either expressing or suppressing it, I just relate to it? I stop the anger and just relate to the thought process?

TR: You don't stop the anger, you just *are* the anger. Anger just hangs out as it is. That is relating with the anger. Then the anger becomes vivid and directionless, and it diffuses into energy. The idea of relating with it has nothing to do with expressing yourself to the other person. The Tibetan expression for that is *rang sar shak,* which means "leave it in its own place." Let anger be in its own place.

STUDENT: I still don't understand what we should try to communicate to a dying person.

TRUNGPA RINPOCHE: You see, death is a very *real* experience. Usually, we do not connect with a sense of reality. If we have an accident—or whatever happens in our lives—we do not regard it as a real experience, even though it may hurt us. It is real to us as far as pain and physical damages are concerned, but still it's not real for us because we immediately look at it in terms of how it could be otherwise. There's always the idea of first aid or some other redeeming aspect of the situation. If you are talking to a dying friend or relative, you should transmit the idea that death is a real experience, rather than that it's just a joke and the person could get better. Often people tell the dying person things like: "Life is really a joke altogether. The great saints say it's not real. Life is unreal. What is death, anyway?" When we try to take this kind of approach, we become jumpy ourselves; and that jumpiness is what we end up communicating to the dying person. We should help them to understand that death is real.

5

The Lion's Roar

WE HAVE LOOKED INTO THE IDEA of timelessness, or eternity. It might be necessary for us now to look a bit further. Conquering or transcending the sense of experience brings us to something completely nondualistic. We might call it sanity. The aspect of Padmasambhava known as Nyima Öser displayed sanity in relating to the concept of time and to ideas or experiences connected with spiritual achievement. Having looked briefly into his example, we might now go ahead and discuss another aspect of Padmasambhava: Shakya Senge, Padmasambhava as buddha.

The principle connected with this aspect of Padmasambhava is that, once one has already conquered any sense of gaining anything in the relative world, one has to go ahead and make a relationship with complete and total sanity, the awakened state of mind. Shakya Senge, Padmasambhava as buddha, is concerned with this. Shakya Senge is not buddha in the hinayana sense but in the mahayana sense. The mahayana style of Padmasambhava has to do with utterance of the lion's roar, which in the mahayana teaching refers to proclaiming the teaching of shunyata, the ultimate sanity.

So, this aspect of Padmasambhava is connected with the expression of the ultimate sanity.

You might ask, "How could this ultimate sanity go further than conquering conceptuality and the sense of experience? Is there something more than that? Isn't that enough?" At this point, there is something more subtle than that. Conquering conceptuality and the sense of experience is a step toward proclamation. First you have to conquer the enemy, then you can proclaim that you have gained victory over him. In making the proclamation referred to as the lion's roar, Padmasambhava as buddha further emphasizes that sanity. The lion's roar is not regarded as a challenge, but as an adornment. It is not a challenge concerning whether the conquering process has been accomplished or not. Rather, when you have already achieved victory, then the victory brings a sense of good news. Proclamation of this good news is the lion's roar.

In connection with Padmasambhava's life, good news is ultimate good news. It is the good news that the spiritual journey need never have been made. The journey has already been completed, therefore there's no point in searching or trying to gain further insights. The needlessness of making the spiritual journey is the good news. That is the lion's roar. This is something much more than what the mahayana sutras talk about. The mahayana sutras talk about attainment of perfect sanity through realizing that form is emptiness and emptiness is form, and so forth. But the lion's roar that we are talking about here is something much more than that. It goes further in that the ultimate good news is independent of any victory. It is ultimate.

What is Padmasambhava's style of manifesting crazy wisdom in this context? He is the universal monarch who looks down over the yanas of the teachings rather than up to them.

According to the story. Padmasambhava studied with Ananda, the attendant and disciple of the Buddha. He was ordained by Ananda as a bhikshu, and he attained understanding of the message of the Buddha. Padmasambhava regarded Ananda, the Buddha's disciple, more as a guru than as a preceptor. That is an important distinction. He regarded him as a guru rather than as a master of discipline, an informant, a professor, or a teacher in the ordinary sense, because Ananda was in the direct lineage of transmission from the Buddha. This meant that working with him involved a living relationship with the teachings.

Padmasambhava's realization here is something we can relate to as well. The sense of dignity that speaks out and expresses that the journey need never have been made is true. The idea that the spiritual journey needs to be made is a deception. From that point of view, even the ten bhumis of the bodhisattva path are a sophistry. Since there are no bhumis at all, how could there be ten of them?

Seeing things in this way is a part of the crazy wisdom of directness, complete directness. It involves directly relating with sanity, or *bodhi* mind, with the experience of the Buddha when he attained vajralike samadhi sitting in the shade of the bodhi tree. It is also a further step toward trusting in buddha-nature. At this point, we cannot even call it buddha-*nature,* because "nature" automatically implies something embryonic. But in this case, we are not talking about something embryonic but about the living Buddha. Padmasambhava associated himself with the Buddha and discovered sanity. He related with Ananda as the messenger who awakened his inspiration.

A guru does not really transmit spiritual entities into us or through us. A guru just reminds us that there is sanity already in us. So Ananda only provided, or for that matter

Padmasambhava only provides, a reminder that things are so in this way.

We might find it difficult to follow what this experience is about or to identify ourselves with it. We might find hearing about this like listening to a story in which such-and-such a thing happened and then after that everybody lived happily ever after. But the story of Padmasambhava should be something more than that. If we actually relate with what happens in the life of Padmasambhava, we will find that it is quite realistic and personal. We acknowledge sanity, and then sanity comes about by itself.

Acknowledging sanity is a discipline or a pretense: you pretend to be the Buddha, you believe you *are* the Buddha. Again, we are not talking about buddha-nature as an embryonic state, but of the living situation of buddhahood having already happened. We adopt such a pretense at the beginning, or maybe we should call it a belief. It is a belief in the sense that our buddhahood is seemingly not real but we take it as a reality. Some element of mind's trickery is necessary. And then we find ourselves having been tricked into enlightenment.

There are all kinds of tricks that exist as part of the teaching process. They are known as *skillful means*. That seems to be something of a euphemism.

Skillful means are part of the spiritual tradition. The lineage gurus' conduct in relating with students is a traditional discipline. Skillful means are necessary, because there is a tendency to run away from sanity of this nature. Students might find sanity too spacious, too irritating. We would prefer a little claustrophobic insanity, snug and comforting insanity. Getting into that is like crawling back into a marsupial's pouch. That's the usual tendency, because acknowledging precision and sanity is too crispy, too cool, too cold. It's too early to wake up; we'd rather go back to bed. Going back to bed is relating to the mind's deceptions, which in fact we prefer. We like to get a little bit confused and set up our homes in that. We don't prefer sanity or enlightenment in fact. That seems to be the problem rather than that we don't have it or can't get it. If we really prefer basic sanity or enlightenment, it's irritatingly possible to get into it.

That seems to have been the approach of Padmasambhava's aspect Shakya Senge: he preferred to become like the Buddha. He went to see Ananda and talked to him about the Buddha. He studied with Ananda, worked with him, and he became buddha. You might say, "That's too quick," but nevertheless, it happened.

Then we have another aspect of Padmasambhava, called Senge Dradrok, which again is connected with the lion's roar. The name actually means "lion's roar" or, more literally, "making a noise like a lion." In this aspect, Padmasambhava manifests as a defender of the faith, a great magician.

At that time in India, there were major incursions of heretics, or *tirthikas,* as they are known in Sanskrit. They were Hindus. They are referred to as heretics because of their belief in duality—in the existence of an external divine being and in the existence of *atman* as the recipient of that divine being.

Of course you might criticize this approach, saying that we all should have high regard for the sacred writings of Hinduism, especially the mystical teachings of Hinduism such as the Vedanta. And actually, the vedantic writings themselves do not quite express things dualistically; they are not quite in the dualistic style of spirituality. But the heretics that Padmasambhava was dealing with were believers in the literal truth of dualism. They misunderstood the real depth of the mystic teachings and believed in an external god and an internal ego. Strangely enough, believing in this kind of separateness can bring about very powerful psychic powers. Miracles of all kinds can be performed, and some technical and intellectual understanding of the teachings can be developed.

In relation to these heretics, Padmasambhava acted as an organic agent, an agent of the natural action of the elements. If you mistreat the fire in your fireplace, your house will catch fire. If you don't pay enough attention while cutting your carrots, you might cut your finger. It is this mindlessness and mistreatment of the natural situation that is the heretical quality. Rather than regarding existing situations of nonduality as they are, you try to interpret them a bit so that they help to maintain your existence. For example, believing in God is a way of making sure that *you* exist. Singing a song of praise to God makes *you* happier, because *you* are singing the song about him. Since there is a good audience, a good recipient, therefore God exists. That kind of approach is heretical from the Buddhist point of view.

At that time, the great Buddhist monasteries in a certain part of India were being challenged by Hindu pandits. The Hindu pandits were coming to the monasteries and teaching, and the monks were rapidly turning into Hindus. It was a tremendous catastrophe. So Padmasambhava was asked to come. Those who invited him said, "We can't seem to match those Hindu pandits intellectually, so please save us by performing some magic for us. Maybe that is the only solution."

Padmasambhava came to live in one of the monasteries. One day, he produced an earthquake by pointing his trident in the direction of the Hindu pandits. There were landslides, and five hundred Hindu pandits were destroyed.

What do you make of that?

When somebody becomes unreasonable, they create their own destruction. By putting it that way, I am not trying to make sure that you are not put off by Padmasambhava and his activities. I am not acting as his spokesman and saying, "He's good anyway, in spite of those actions of his." It is simply that with him acting as the agent of the elements, of the organic process, the unreasonable and man-made element had to be diminished.

People in Bhutan were recently trying to build a road from India to Bhutan, called the Bhutan National Highway. They were building and building. They had bulldozers and they had Indian road-making experts. They spent millions and millions of rupees, and they built a beautiful road. But when the rainy season came, the whole road was swept away by tremendous landslides. By building a road you interfere with the mountain, with the structure of the rock. As the only possible reaction of nature to that disturbance, landslides develop. Then once again there is another project requiring millions of rupees, and this process goes on and on.

The last time it happened was when the president of India was paying a state visit to Bhutan. The airplane that was carrying India's gifts to the Bhutanese king and government got lost in the mist and crashed in the Bhutanese mountains. And as the Indian president was preparing to return to India, sudden landslides took place as a farewell gesture to him.

I'm not saying that the president of India is a heretic, but the definition of heresy here is very delicate. If you are not in tune with the nature of reality, you are making yourself into a target, an extra satellite. And there's no one to feed you. There's no fuel for you except your own resources, and you are bound to die because you can't keep regenerating without further resources. That is what happened to the pandits whom Padmasambhava killed. This is very uncompassionate or outrageous, but Padmasambhava in this case is representing the nature of reality rather than acting as a black magician or white magician.

It seems that we cannot be instructed how to perform acts such as the destruction of the pandits. Although the teachings have been handed down through generations and generations without interruption or perversion, so that even now we possess the complete teachings of Padmasambhava, none of those teachings talk about how to kill heretics. There are no such teachings. But the teachings do talk about how to work with practice and your attitude toward it organically. You do that, and the perverters of the teachings destroy themselves. That seems to be the basic message here. That seems to be the aspect of Padmasambhava called "Lion's Roar," Senge Dradrok.

STUDENT: Will the elements also organically protect those who don't pervert the teachings?

TRUNGPA RINPOCHE: Maybe.

STUDENT: Is Padmasambhava's organic action in connection with the elements the same as the action of the *dharmapalas*, the protectors of the teachings?

TRUNGPA RINPOCHE: Somewhat, yes. But it is also more than the action of the dharmapalas. The dharmapalas are just sort of reminders. But in this case, there is a complete message.

S: Isn't what you are calling the "action of the elements" or "a complete message" in a sense just karmic action?

TR: It is karmic action in the sense that there is an organic thing happening, but there's also something specially organic, which has the quality of being deliberate. There seem to be two patterns. There is a difference between a landslide occurring in the area of a coal mine and the landslide that happened in the heretics' home.

STUDENT: This business of tricking yourself into being buddha is not at all clear to me. It sounds so un-Buddhist to use your mind to trick yourself. Is that different from what you talk about as deception, as conning yourself, conning experience?

TRUNGPA RINPOCHE: It's quite different. The deception of conning yourself has to be based on elaborate strategies. Tricking yourself into becoming buddha is immediate. It happens on the spot.

S: But if I say to myself, "I am buddha" when I don't really know what buddha is—

TR: It doesn't really matter. That's the whole point—we don't know what buddha is. And maybe not knowing what buddha is, is buddha.

S: Well, it doesn't seem like you actually do anything then. Do you do something?

TR: It's up to you. You have to develop your own system.

S: Does it differ from just confidence?

TR: Yes. It's a quick switch, as if the carpet were being pulled out from under your feet. Or your feet were being pulled over the carpet. It's true. It can be done.

S: It's like tripping-out then?

TR: Tripping-out takes a lot of preparation. But if you are tricked, it takes you by surprise, as though nothing had happened.

S: Is that connected with visualizations and mantra practice?

TR: It's something much more immediate than that. It's

just a change of attitude. Instead of trying to become buddha, you suddenly realize that buddha is trying to become
you.

S: Does this have anything to do with an *abhisheka*, an em-
powerment?

TR: I think so, yes. That's what's called the fourth
abhisheka, the sudden introduction of nowness.

S: It seems that there's a whole process of preparation
that's necessary for this shift in perspective to take place.

TR: You have to be willing to do that. That's liberation.
Apart from that, there is nothing more. It's a question of
your being willing to do it; that's the important point. You
have to be willing to commit yourself to go through the dis-
comforts that might occur after you are buddha.

STUDENT: Earlier you talked about eternity and Padmasambhava being turned into a HUM. Would being turned
into a HUM be like a death experience? Would you have to
dissolve in order to penetrate experience; would you have
to die?

TRUNGPA RINPOCHE: Penetration is not particularly
connected with death. Being turned into a HUM is becoming
an intense person. You become a capsulized being. You are
reduced to a capsule, a very concentrated sense of being
yourself. You are just a grain of sand. It is not dissolving but
being intensified into one dot.

S: When Shri Simha swallowed Padmasambhava and shat
him out, was that still him?

TR: Naturally. The analogy is swallowing a diamond.
When you shit it out, it's still a genuine diamond.

STUDENT: Penetration seems to involve a sense of sharpness. You're in the midst of an egoistic manipulation, and
then something wakes you up with a kind of sharpness.

TRUNGPA RINPOCHE: The sharpness that cuts through neurotic mind seems to be like a two-edged razor that cuts in both directions simultaneously, so the only thing that exists is the sharpness itself. It's not like a needle, not like an axe. It cuts both the projection and the projector at the same time. That is why there is a craziness aspect: the user gets cut by that razor as well as what he is using it on. That makes it humorous, too. Nobody wins the battle. The enemy gets destroyed and the defender gets destroyed as well—simultaneously—so it's very crazy. Usually if you're fighting against something, you're supposed to win, but in this case you don't. Both sides get destroyed. Nobody wins. In other words, both win.

STUDENT: This seems to be connected with shunyata. There could be a gap at any instant, and then there seems to be another kind of sharpness—

TRUNGPA RINPOCHE: That's quite different. When there's a sense of gap, there's no blade to cut anything. It's self-perpetuating in the sense of HUM. From that point of view, the shunyata experience and crazy wisdom are different. Compared to crazy wisdom, shunyata provides a home, a mutual home, a comfortable home, whereas crazy wisdom provides a constant cutting process. The tantric approach is related with energy; the shunyata experience is just wisdom alone, wisdom without energy. It's a discovery, an experience, a nest of some kind.

STUDENT: What was Padmasambhava's motivation in wanting to become buddha? I'm thinking of what you said earlier: we don't want that uncomfortable state; we want the comfort of claustrophobia and insanity.

TRUNGPA RINPOCHE: Yes. I suppose as far as samsaric mind is concerned, it's a perverted motivation. It is going against that tendency of wanting a home. It goes against the grain of what our parents always say to us: "Don't you want to get married and have a job and a comfortable home instead of just sitting and meditating?"

S: But is there some motivation that is not from the samsaric point of view, but that exists in its own right?

TR: Outlandishness. Being uncivilized.

S: Is that a part of ourselves that we could discover or cultivate in some way?

TR: That's what we have to see. That's what we have to find out. There's no prescription.

S: Is this outlandishness something that we already experience occasionally as part of our lives or something we haven't experienced yet?

TR: I don't know. Let's find out.

STUDENT: Is what you said before about buddha trying to become you—is that the motivating factor?

TRUNGPA RINPOCHE: Well, there is something very strange going on. You are absolutely comfortable and happy the way you are, yet at the same time you find it excruciatingly painful. You are not certain whether you want to stay the way you are, which is very pleasurable, or not stay the way you are, because it is very painful at the same time. That kind of pushing and pulling happens all the time. That seems to be the motivation. You want to keep your habitual patterns, but at the same time you find them too monotonous—that's the kind of motivation. I mean, we cannot define that as being something special. We cannot say you are making a journey in some particular direction. The directions are confused. You are *not* confused about whether you are coming or going, but you *still* want to do something about the situation. That is the contagious quality of bud-dha-nature, which is trying to shine through all the time, seemingly.

Loden Choksi

6

Intellect and Working with Negativity

THE NEXT ASPECT OF PADMASAMBHAVA is actually called Padmasambhava. For some strange reason, "Padmasambhava" became popular as the general name for all the iconographical aspects of this figure. Maybe a certain Gelukpa influence crept into the naming process. Followers of Padmasambhava in Tibet usually refer to him as Guru Rinpoche or Pema Jungne, "the Lotus-Born," which is Padmakara in Sanskrit. Padmasambhava is then the name of only one of the aspects. It seems this has something to do with a sectarian squabble in which one party holds that Padmasambhava is not a cosmic principle, but just a pandit named Padmasambhava.

In any case, the particular aspect known as Padmasambhava was a pandit, a scholar. He entered Nalanda University and studied what is known as the threefold discipline: meditation, morality, and knowledge, or learning. Those three disciplines correspond to the three sections of the Buddhist scripture called the Tripitaka. One section of the Tripitaka discusses monastic discipline, another the basic teachings of the sutras, and the third the psychological structure of beings.

People frequently ask, "Wouldn't it be possible on the spiritual path not to do any studying at all? Can't we just meditate a lot and learn everything from our experiences?" Many people believe that if you sit and meditate a lot, you don't have to read scriptures or study anything at all. They say that just by meditating everything will come to you. That approach seems to be one-sided. It leaves no room for sharpening the intellect or for disciplining the mind. It also does not take into account the knowledge that protects us from indulging in states of absorption, knowledge that tells us that it is necessary to let go of particular states and bring ourselves into another frame of mind. Study and scholastic learning play an extremely important part for us. This is what is demonstrated by Padmasambhava in his pandit aspect.

One of the problems connected with intellect and intellectual understanding is that if we look for and come up with answers, conclusions, logical deductions, we tend to end up with a high opinion of our understanding. If we develop that, then we may no longer be able to experience things properly or learn anything more from the teachings at all. We become hardened scholars and bookworms. We might begin to feel that practices are unsafe if we do not know what they are, so we have to study them scholastically first. This attitude might go as far as saying that if you really want to study the Buddhist teachings, first you have to learn Sanskrit as well as Japanese or Tibetan. You can't even begin to practice meditation until you have learned those languages and studied the appropriate texts.

This attitude suggests that the student should become a superscholar. When the student has become an extremely perfect scholar, he has attained buddhahood. He has all the

answers; he knows everything inside out. This kind of om-
niscience, according to this view, makes one a buddha.

This view that the enlightened being is a learned person,
a great scholar, is a misunderstanding, another extreme. Enlightenment is not purely a matter of collecting information.
If a buddha didn't know how to change his snow tires, for
example, a person with this view might begin to have
doubts about him. After all, he is supposed to be the omnis-
cient one; how could he be a buddha if he doesn't know how
to do that? The perfect buddha would be able to surprise
you with his knowledge in every area. He would be a good
cook, a good mechanic, a good scientist, a good poet, a
good musician—he would be good at everything. That is a
diluted and diffused idea of buddha, to say the least. He is
not that kind of universal expert, nor a superprofessor.

But if the proper idea of intellectual understanding and
sharpening the intellect is not feeding oneself millions of
bits of information and making oneself into a walking library, then what is it? It is connected with developing
sharpness and precision in relating with the nature of reality.
This has nothing to do with dwelling on logical conclusions
or concepts. One has to have a neutral attitude in one's intellectual study of the teaching, one that is neither purely
critical nor purely devotional. One doesn't try to come to
conclusions. The purpose of study, rather than to come to
conclusions, is to experience things logically and sensibly.
This seems to be the middle way [between the two extremes
of rejecting the intellect and emphasizing it exclusively].

Becoming accomplished in intellectual study usually
means forming strong opinions. If you are a scholar, your
name becomes worth mentioning if you have made some intellectual discovery. But what we are talking about here is
not exactly discovery in the professorial sense, but rather
discovery on the level of examining and dealing with per-

sonal experience. Through such a process, your personal experience is worked through—it is beaten, burned, and hammered as in working with gold, to use a scriptural analogy. In dealing with your experience, you eat, you chew, and you finally swallow and digest. In this way, the *whole thing* becomes workable; your focus is not purely on highlights, such as developing your personality into that of a great learned person—a Buddhologist or a Tibetologist or something like that.

In other words, intellect here means absence of watcher. If we watch ourselves learning—watch ourselves growing, developing, becoming more and more scholastic people—then we are comparing ourselves with "other." We are constantly gaining weight in our egos, because we are comparing ourselves with "other." Whereas if there is experience or intellectual study going on without a watcher, it becomes very simple and direct. This kind of intellect without watcher has qualities similar to what we were describing earlier in connection with the experience of the young prince. It is open, willing to explore. It is without a particular attitude. It is without a sense that you want what is happening to be replaced by something else, that you want your ignorance to be replaced by information. It is a constant discovery of new situations in life and what the teachings and scriptures have to say about them. It means discovering the subtleties and feelings related with different aspects of Buddhism. It means understanding the whole geography of the teachings, so that you are not bewildered by some new approach, some new wisdom. You are not bewildered, because you know what area of human psychology a particular approach is connected with. In this way, whatever comes up in relation to the teaching becomes very simple, very easy and workable. This was the practice exemplified by Padmasambhava as Padmasambhava. He became a great pandit because he worked with his intellect without a watcher. On the basis of his example, we can also work with intellect without a watcher.

You might ask: "If there is no watcher, how do we know that we have understood what we have learned?" But it is possible to approach learning and understanding other than by collecting information for the sake of gaining a new personality, or developing a new ego. That is not the only way. There are other ways for one to be highly scholastic, highly intellectual. It is possible to do that without a watcher.

Another aspect of Padmasambhava is known as Loden Choksi, who was a *rajguru,* as they call the spiritual teacher of a royal family in India. The way Loden Choksi came to be a rajguru is an interesting story. He was wandering from place to place when he came to a nunnery. He began instructing the head nun there, who was the princess of the kingdom of Sahor. Sahor was somewhere in the area of Himachal Pradesh in present-day northern India. The princess was very precious for this kingdom, because she had been invited to become the queen of a number of neighboring kingdoms, as well as of important kingdoms like China, Persia, and, according to the story, the Roman Empire. Despite these invitations, the princess refused to have anything to do with worldly power and pleasures. She wanted to become a Buddhist nun, and she did. The king of Sahor was extremely fearful that if the princess was not successful in maintaining her nunhood [this would be regarded as a deception and a political affront by those kingdoms whose invitations she had rejected and] that they might attack his kingdom. [Therefore, the king surrounded her with five hundred nuns to guard her in her discipline.]

So Padmasambhava was there giving teachings to the princess and the five hundred nuns when a local cowherd passed by and heard a man's voice coming out of the nunnery. Word of this spread throughout the kingdom and created a huge scandal. At some point, the king and queen and their ministers heard the story. They hoped to be able to expose the scandal as based on a false rumor, but were unable to track down the cowherd who was the original witness. They had a collection of lots of gifts placed at the entrance to the royal courtyard and let it be known that if the original witness would come forward and tell his story, he would receive all these gifts. There was gold, silver, jewelry, silks, and so on. Finally, the herdsman appeared and told his story, which actually seemed to be true. He had no ulterior motive for spreading a scandal in the kingdom.

The king sent one of his ministers to find out what was happening at the nunnery. The minister found the doors completely locked, and the nuns would not let anyone inside, even if it was a messenger from the king who just wanted to inspect. The king suspected that something funny was going on at the nunnery and sent his soldiers to break in. They did so and found Padmasambhava sitting on the throne in the assembly hall, instructing the nuns.

The soldiers tried to seize Padmasambhava but found it very difficult, bewilderingly difficult, to get hold of him. They couldn't catch him at all. At this point the king became extremely upset and angry and sent a huge number of troops to the nunnery. The troops finally captured Padmasambhava and all the nuns.

The traditional means of execution of this country was burning the prisoner alive in a sandalwood fire. So they put Padmasambhava in a sandalwood fire, and the princess was put into a dungeon filled with thorns. The sandalwood fire, which usually died after twenty-four hours, continued to burn for a long time. With other criminals there was usually no difficulty, but in this case the fire continued to burn and smoke for about three weeks. The king and the people began to wonder what the problem was. Could it be possible that there was something unusual about this wanderer they had burned? The king decided he wanted to collect some pieces of this wanderer's bones in case they might have interesting magical properties. He sent a messenger to the place where the fire was, and the messenger found that a huge lake had appeared on the spot, with logs still aflame around the edges of it. In the middle of this lake was a lotus flower with Padmasambhava sitting on it.

The king realized he had made a big mistake and began speaking to Padmasambhava. Padmasambhava sang a song, saying, "Welcome to the great sinner, welcome to the king trapped in confusion," and so forth. The king invited Padmasambhava to come to his palace. Padmasambhava finally accepted his invitation. At this point, according to the story, Padmasambhava conducted sadhana practices of the *vajradhatu* mandala at the king's palace. The result, according to the story, is that the kingdom was completely emptied out in seven years' time. The whole civilization dissolved as people became great yogis and found there was no point in sticking to ordinary domestic work. They all became crazy.

In this story, Loden Choksi, the rajguru aspect of Padmasambhava, performed a miracle. His miracle was not merely converting the king; the miracle was his manner of dealing with whatever threats or accusations arose. Loden Choksi manifested the invincibility of Padmasambhava. Any challenge to him, rather than being viewed as a threat, turned into a further adornment of his action. Using obstacles as a way of working with life situations plays a very important part in crazy wisdom.

This may be a familiar idea for people already exposed to the teachings of crazy wisdom, but for most people, who think of spirituality as based purely on goodness, any kind of opposition or obstacle is considered a manifestation of evil. Regarding obstacles as adornments is quite an unusual idea. If there is a threat to the teacher or the teaching, it tends to be categorized immediately as the "work of the devil." In this view, the idea is to try not to relate to the obstacles or threats, but to cast them out as something bad, something antagonistic to the teaching. You should just purify yourself of this work of the devil. You should abandon it, rather than exploring it as part of the organic and integral development of the situation you are working with. You regard it purely as a problem.

I suppose if those of us already familiar with these teachings would look into ourselves on a very subtle level, we might still find some element of this approach. Although we know the philosophy and the ideas—we know we are supposed to work with negativity and use it as an adornment—nevertheless there is still some sense of trying to find alternatives, of trying to find some kind of underlying promise.

Actually, this happens quite a lot with our students. People talk about relating to negativity as part of the development of the situation, but then they regard this approach in itself as an alternative way of solving the problem of negativity. Even older students are constantly asking questions, publicly and in private, based on this alternative-solution approach. They still believe that there is a "best way"; they still believe there is a way to some kind of happiness. Although we know we are supposed to relate to pain and misery as part of the path, we still try to regard *that* as a way to happiness, as a way of solving the problem, as a better alternative. If we had been Padmasambhava as the rajguru, we would have tried to talk to the guards who arrested us before they put us in the fire. We would have said: "This is a great mistake; you mustn't do this. You don't understand what you're doing." We would try this, rather than letting the event happen, rather than letting action speak louder than words.

There still seems to be some kind of timidity in our general approach. We are timid in the sense that, no matter how subtle or obvious the teachings may be, we are still not reconciled to the notion that "pain and pleasure alike are ornaments which it is pleasant to wear."[6] We might read it, we might say it, but still we find it magnificent to twist the twist and feel that misery or negativity is good: "We have to work with it. Okay, I've been doing that. Lately I've been finding all kinds of rough and rugged things going on in my mind and in my life. It's not particularly pleasant, but all in all it's *interesting* for me." There is some tinge of hope. The idea of finding the negativity "interesting" is that somehow as we go along we will be saved. The unspoken implication is that finally the whole thing is going to be good and pleasurable. It's very subtle. It is almost as though there's an unspoken agreement that in the end all roads are going to lead to Rome.

We are still struggling along with the hinayana mentality, even though we are talking about the most profound teachings of crazy wisdom. We are still thinking this crazy wisdom might lead us to happiness, that the crutches of the vajrayana might help us to walk on a good hinayana path. This shows that we have not related to the whole thing as hopeless—absolutely hopeless—at all. Even hopelessness has been regarded as a solution. That cop-out is still happening. We are still going on as though there were this silent agreement that, no matter what we say, we are working toward some kind of happiness. But Padmasambhava in his aspect of rajguru was not concerned about that at all. His approach was, "Let happiness present *itself* if it happens, but in the meantime, let me be executed if necessary."

Acknowledge yourself as the criminal—go ahead and do

it! He did it. He was executed as a criminal. But then something changed.

Acknowledging other people's mistakes as yours seems to be very difficult to do; however, pain is the path. We don't want to get blamed for somebody else's action. We will immediately say that we didn't do it. "It wasn't my fault." We can't bear to be blamed unjustly. Well, that is quite sensible, I suppose—people don't like to be blamed. But suppose we decide to take the whole thing on ourselves and let ourselves be blamed, then what would happen? It would be very interesting to find out—purely by following the example of Padmasambhava (if that makes you feel any better).

That is a very interesting kind of approach. It is not particularly subtle; it is obvious. It becomes subtle only with the twist of the twist of the twist of deception, which is a twist toward a goal.

STUDENT: I'd like to know a little bit more about this twist of deception.

TRUNGPA RINPOCHE: Well, we could speak about it a lot, but the main point seems to be to cut the self-justification of "It's going to be okay, there's some kind of promise of a reward *anyway.*" Even believing in no promise is a promise of some kind. That kind of twist is always there. And unless we are willing to get blamed unjustly, we can't cut our deception at all. Which is very difficult to do. We are willing to lie for ourselves, but we are not willing to lie for the sake of others. We are not at all willing to take somebody else's pain. Unless maybe we talk to the people whose pain we are taking and say, "Look, I'm doing a good job for you; this is all for you." You feel you would like to have a word with that person before you give in.

STUDENT: Padmasambhava is the lion of the dharma. Somebody wants to blame him for his own bad action. Padmasambhava says, "Sure, go ahead, blacken my name." I don't understand that exactly. Maybe if that was the only thing he could do, it would make sense, but it seems there are other modes of action available. He could pacify, enrich, magnetize, and so on. But just going along with the misplaced blame seems almost like avoiding the situation. I don't see the intelligent quality of his behaving as he did in that situation.

TRUNGPA RINPOCHE: In this case, because he didn't try to magnetize, the whole thing became more powerful. Instead he gave in, but he gave in in such a powerful way that the others automatically got rebounds from the situation. The result was that in fact Padmasambhava didn't have to talk himself out of his situation, but the others had to do it for him.

The message to us as followers of his is that, since we don't use such techniques too often (to say the least), it is worth trying to practice this approach. We don't have to conceptualize and say that giving in to the situation is the *only* way. That is not the point. We have all the riches and wealth of all kinds of techniques, and this one is also one of the interesting ones. It is worth looking at. I mean, you have eight styles for dealing with your life—Padmasambhava's eight aspects each have different messages—and this is one of them.

STUDENT: Was giving in in this way what Christ did? Just permitting his situation to happen?

TRUNGPA RINPOCHE: That seems to be very obvious, yes. He just took the blame.

STUDENT: I don't understand the idea of not avoiding pain. If we are not trying to avoid pain then what is the meaning of the Noble Truth about the cessation of pain?

TRUNGPA RINPOCHE: Here the cessation of pain is the sense of seeing the pain from a reverse angle—from behind—rather than eliminating it.

S: You mean you just end up on the other side of the pain?

TR: Yes, [on the other side of] the creator of the pain, which is confusion.

STUDENT: It seems that both Christ and Padmasambhava had to use magic in order to achieve their final victory.

TRUNGPA RINPOCHE: Not necessarily. It might have become magic by itself.

S: I mean the lake, and sitting in the lotus flower and—

TR: That was not magic particularly. That was just what happened. And for that matter, the resurrection could be said not to have been magic at all. It's just what happened in the case of Christ.

S: It's magical in the sense that it's very unusual. I mean, if that isn't magic, what is?

TR: Well, in that case what we're doing here is magic. We are doing something extremely unusual, for America. It happens to have developed by itself. We couldn't have created the whole situation. Our getting together and discussing this subject just happened by itself.

STUDENT: Rinpoche, what you were saying about using pain as an adornment seemed to me like the difference between collecting information and really experiencing the implications of it. But I don't see how you can be sure that you are really making contact with your experience.

TRUNGPA RINPOCHE: One shouldn't regard the whole thing as a way of getting ahead of ego. Just relate to it as an ongoing process. Don't do anything with it, just go on. It's a very casual matter.

STUDENT: What does Loden Choksi mean?

TRUNGPA RINPOCHE: *Loden* means "possessing intelligence"; *choksi* means "supreme world" or "supreme existence." In this case, the name does not seem to be as significant as with some of the other aspects. It is not nearly as vivid as, for example, Senge Dradrok or Dorje Trolö. *Loden Choksi* has something to do with being skillful.

STUDENT: What is the difference between the kind of direct intellectual perception you were talking about here and other kinds of perception?

TRUNGPA RINPOCHE: It seems that if you are purely looking for answers, then you don't perceive anything. In the proper use of intellect, you don't look for answers, you just see; you just take notes in your mind. And even then, you don't have the goal of collecting information; you just relate to what is there as an expression of intelligence. That way your intelligence can't be conned by extraneous suggestions. Rather, you have sharpened your intellect and you can relate directly to what is happening.

S: But how would you differentiate that from other kinds of perception?

TR: In general, we have perceptions with all kinds of things mixed in; that is, we have conditioned perceptions which contain a purpose of magnetizing or destroying. Such perceptions contain passion and aggression and all the rest of it. There are ulterior motives of all kinds, as opposed to just seeing clearly, just looking at things very precisely, sharply.

Dorje Trolö

7

Dorje Trolö and the Three Styles of Transmission

THE EIGHTH ASPECT OF PADMASAMBHAVA is Dorje Trolö, the final and absolute aspect of crazy wisdom. To discuss this eighth aspect of Padmasambhava, we have to have some background knowledge about [traditional] ways of communicating the teachings. The idea of *lineage* is associated with the transmission of the message of *adhishthana,* which means "energy" or, if you like, "grace." This is transmitted like an electric current from the trikaya guru to sentient beings. In other words, crazy wisdom is a continual energy that flows and that, as it flows, regenerates itself. The only way to regenerate this energy is by radiating or communicating it, by putting it into practice or acting it out. It is unlike other energies, which, when you use them, move toward cessation or extinction. The energy of crazy wisdom regenerates itself through the process of our living it. As you live this energy, it regenerates itself; you don't live for death but you live for birth. Living is a constant birth process rather than a wearing-out process.

The lineage has three styles of transmitting this energy.

The first is called the *kangsaknyen-gyü*. Here the energy of the lineage is transmitted by word of mouth using ideas and concepts. In some sense this is a crude or primitive method, a somewhat dualistic approach. However, in this case the dualistic approach is functional and worthwhile.

If you sit cross-legged as if you were meditating, the chances are you might actually find yourself meditating after a while. This is like achieving sanity by pushing yourself to imitate it, by behaving as though you were sane already. In the same way, it is possible to use words, terms, images, and ideas—teaching orally or in writing—as though they were an absolutely perfect means of transmission. The procedure is to present an idea, then the refutation of [the opposite of] that idea, and then to associate the idea with an authentic scripture or teaching that has been given in the past.

Believing in the sacredness of certain things on a primitive level is the first step in transmission. Traditionally, scriptures or holy books are not to be trodden upon, sat upon, or otherwise mistreated, because very powerful things are said in them. The idea is that by mistreating the books, you mistreat the messages they contain. This is a way of believing in some kind of entity, or energy, or force—in the living quality of something.

The second style of communicating, or teaching, is the *rigdzin da-gyü*. This is the method of crazy wisdom, but on the relative level, not the absolute level. Here you communicate by creating incidents that seem to happen by themselves. Such incidents are seemingly blameless, but they do have an instigator somewhere. In other words, the guru tunes himself in to the cosmic energy, or whatever you would like to call it. Then if there is a need to create chaos, he directs his attention toward chaos. And quite appropriately, chaos presents itself, as if it happened by accident or mistake. *Da* in Tibetan means "symbol" or "sign." The sense of this is that the crazy-wisdom guru does not speak or teach on the ordinary level, but rather, he or she creates a symbol, or means. A symbol in this case is not like something that stands for something else, but it is something that presents the living quality of life and creates a message out of it.

The third one is called *gyalwa gong-gyü*. *Gong gyü* means "thought lineage" or "mind lineage." From the point of view of the thought lineage, even the method of creating situations is crude, or primitive. Here a mutual understanding takes place that creates a general atmosphere—and the message is understood. If the guru of crazy wisdom is an authentic being, then the authentic communication happens, and the means of communication is neither words nor symbols. Rather, just by being, a sense of precision is communicated. Maybe it takes the form of waiting—for nothing. Maybe it takes pretending to meditate together, but not doing anything. For that matter, it might involve having a very casual relationship: discussing the weather and the flavor of tea; how to make curry, chop suey, or macrobiotic cuisine; or talking about history, or the history of the neighbors—whatever.

The crazy wisdom of the thought lineage takes a form that is somewhat disappointing to the eager recipient of the teachings. You might go and pay a visit to the guru, which you have especially prepared for, and he isn't even interested in talking to you. He's busy reading the newspaper. Or for that matter, he might create "black air," a certain intensity that makes the whole environment threatening. And there's nothing happening—nothing happening to such an extent that you walk out with a sense of relief, glad you didn't have to be there any longer. But then something happens to you as if everything did happen during those periods of silence or intensity.

The thought lineage is more of a presence than something happening. Also, it has an extraordinarily ordinary quality.

In traditional abhishekas, or initiation ceremonies, the energy of the thought lineage is transmitted into your system at the level of the fourth abhisheka. At that point, the guru will ask you suddenly, "What is your name?" or "Where is your mind?" This abrupt question momentarily cuts through your subconscious gossip, creating a bewilderment of a different type [from the type already going on in your mind]. You search for an answer and realize you do have a name and he wants to know it. It is as if you were nameless before, but have now discovered that you have a name. It is that kind of an abrupt moment.

Of course, such ceremonies are subject to corruption. If the teacher is purely following the scriptures and commentaries, and the student is eagerly expecting something powerful, then both the teacher and the student miss the boat simultaneously.

Thought-lineage communication is the teaching of the dharmakaya; the communication by signs and symbols—creating situations—is the sambhogakaya level of teaching; and the communication by words is the nirmanakaya level of teaching. Those are the three styles in which the crazy-wisdom guru communicates to the potential crazy-wisdom student.

The whole thing is not as outrageous as it may seem. Nevertheless, there is an undercurrent of taking advantage of the mischievousness of reality, and this creates a sense of craziness or a sense that something or other is not too solid. Your sense of security is under attack. So the recipient of crazy wisdom—the ideal crazy-wisdom student—should feel extremely insecure, threatened. That way you manufacture half of the crazy wisdom and the guru manufactures the other half. Both the guru and the student are alarmed by the situation. Your mind has nothing to work on. A sudden gap has been created—bewilderment.

This kind of bewilderment is quite different from the bewilderment of ignorance. This is the bewilderment that happens between the question and the answer. It is the boundary between the question and the answer. There is a question, and you are just about to answer that question: there is a gap. You have oozed out your question, and the answer hasn't come through yet. There is already a feeling of a sense of the answer, a sense that something positive is happening—but nothing has happened yet. There is that point where the answer is just about to be born and the question has just died.

There is very strange chemistry there; the combination of the death of the question and the birth of the answer creates uncertainty. It is intelligent uncertainty—sharp, inquisitive. This is unlike ego's bewilderment of ignorance, which has totally and completely lost touch with reality because you have given birth to duality and are uncertain about how to handle the next step. You are bewildered because of ego's approach of duality. But in this case it is not bewilderment in the sense of not knowing what to do, but bewilderment because something is just about to happen and hasn't happened yet.

The crazy wisdom of Dorje Trolö is not reasonable but somewhat heavy-handed, because wisdom does not permit compromise. If you compromise between black and white, you come out with a grey color—not quite white and not quite black. It is a sad medium rather than a happy medium—disappointing. You feel sorry that you've let it be compromised. You feel totally wretched that you have compromised. That is why crazy wisdom does not know any compromise. The style of crazy wisdom is to build you up:

build up your ego to the level of absurdity, to the point of comedy, to a point that is bizarre—and then suddenly let you go. So you have a big fall, like Humpty Dumpty: "All the king's horses and all the king's men / Couldn't put Humpty Dumpty together again."

To get back to the story of Padmasambhava as Dorje Trolö, he was asked by a local deity in Tibet, "What frightens you the most?" Padmasambhava said, "I'm frightened of neurotic sin." It so happens that the Tibetan word for sin— *dikpa*—is also the word for scorpion, so the local deity thought he could frighten Padmasambhava by manifesting himself as a giant scorpion. The local deity was reduced to dust—as a scorpion.

Tibet is supposedly ringed by snow-capped mountains, and there are twelve goddesses associated with those mountains who are guardians of the country. When Dorje Trolö came to Tibet, one of those goddesses refused to surrender to him. She ran away from him—she ran all over the place. She ran up a mountain thinking she was running away from Padmasambhava and found him already there ahead of her, dancing on the mountaintop. She ran away down a valley and found Padmasambhava already at the bottom, sitting at the confluence of that valley and the neighboring one. No matter where she ran, she couldn't get away. Finally she decided to jump into a lake and hide there. Padmasambhava turned the lake into boiling iron, and she emerged as a kind of skeleton being. Finally, she had to surrender, because Padmasambhava was everywhere. It was extremely claustrophic in some way.

One of the expressions of crazy wisdom is that you can't get away from it. It's everywhere (whatever "it" is).

At Taktsang in Bhutan, Padmasambhava manifested as Dorje Trolö. He transformed his consort Yeshe Tsogyal into a pregnant tigress, and he roamed about the Taktsang hills riding on this pregnant tigress. His manifesting this way had to do with subduing the psychic energies of the country, a country that was infested with primitive beliefs concerning ego and God.

Another expression of crazy wisdom is controlling psychic energies. The way to control psychic energies is not to create a greater psychic energy and try to dominate them. That just escalates the war, and it becomes too expensive—like the Vietnam War. You come up with a counterstrategy and then there is a counter-counterstrategy and then a counter-counter-counterstrategy. So the idea is not to create a super-power. The way to control the psychic energy of primitive beliefs is to instigate chaos. Introduce confusion among those energies, confuse people's logic. Confuse them so that they have to think twice. That is like the moment of the changing of the guards. At that moment when they begin to think twice, the energy of crazy wisdom zaps out.

Dorje Trolö controlled the psychic energies of primitive beliefs by creating confusion. He was half-Indian and half-Tibetan, an Indian-looking person dressed up as a Tibetan madman. He held a vajra and a dagger, flames shot from his body, and he rode a pregnant tigress. It was quite strange. He was not quite a local deity and not quite a conventional guru. He was neither warrior nor king. He was certainly not an ordinary person. Riding on a tiger is regarded as a mistake, but somehow he managed to accomplish it. Was he trying to disguise himself as a Tibetan, or what was he trying to do? He was not particularly teaching anything. You couldn't deal with him as a Pön priest or a missionary. He wasn't converting anybody; that didn't seem to be his style either. He was just instigating chaos all over the place as he went along. Even the local deities were confused—absolutely upset.

When Padmasambhava went to Tibet, the Indians got

very alarmed. They felt they were losing something very precious, since it seemed he had decided to give his teachings of crazy wisdom only to the Tibetans. This was a terrible insult for the Indians. They prided themselves on being the supreme Aryans, the most intelligent race, the ones most receptive to high teachings. And now instead of teaching them, Padmasambhava was going to the savage country of Tibet, beyond the border areas; he had decided to teach the Tibetans instead of them. King Surya Simha of Uttar Pradesh, the central province of India, sent three *acharyas,* or spiritual masters, to the king of Tibet with a polite message saying that this so-called Padmasambhava was a charlatan, a black magician in fact. The Indian king advised that Padmasambhava was too dangerous for the Tibetans to have in their country and that they should send him back.

The interesting point here is that the teachings of crazy wisdom can only be taught in savage countries, where there is more opportunity to take advantage of chaos, or speed—or whatever you would like to call that factor.

The crazy-wisdom character of Padmasambhava as Dorje Trolö is that of a guru who is unwilling to compromise with anything. If you stand in his way, you are asking for destruction. If you have doubts about him, he takes advantage of your doubts. If you are too devotional or too dependent on blind faith, he will shock you. He takes the ironical aspect of the world very seriously. He plays practical jokes on a larger scale—devastating ones.

The symbolism of the tiger is also interesting. It is connected with the idea of flame, with fire and smoke. And a pregnant tigress is supposed to be the most vicious of all tigers. She is hungry, slightly crazy, completely illogical. You cannot read her psychology and work with it reasonably. She is quite likely to eat you up at any time. That is the nature of Dorje Trolö's transport, his vehicle. The crazy-wisdom guru rides on dangerous energy, impregnated with all kinds of possibilities. This tiger could be said to represent skillful means, crazy skillful means. And Dorje Trolö, who is crazy wisdom, rides on it. They make an excellent couple.

There is another side to Padmasambhava in Tibet, one that is not part of the eight aspects. For Tibetans, Padmasambhava is a father figure. As such, he is usually referred to as Guru Rinpoche, "*the* guru." He fell in love with the Tibetans and lavished tremendous care on them (not exactly the same way the missionaries fell in love with the Africans). The Tibetans were thought of as stupid. They were too faithful and too practical. Therefore, there was a tremendous opening for introducing the craziness of impracticality: abandon your farm, abandon your livelihood, roam about in the mountains dressed in those funny yogic costumes.

Once the Tibetans began to accept those things as acts of sanity, they made excellent yogis, because their approach to yogic practice was also very practical. As they had farmed faithfully and taken care of their herds faithfully, they followed the yogic calling faithfully as well.

The Tibetans were not artistic like the Japanese. Rather, they were excellent farmers, excellent merchants, excellent magicians. The Pön tradition of Tibet was very earthy. It was purely concerned with the realities of life. Pön ceremonies are also sometimes very practical ones. One of the sacred ceremonies involves making a campfire up in the mountains—which keeps you warm. It seems that the deviousness Tibetans have shown in the course of the political intrigues of the twentieth century is entirely out of character. This kind of corruption and political intrigue came to Tibet from the outside—from the Aryan philosophers of India and from the imperial politicians of China.

Padmasambhava's approach was a very beautiful one, and his prophecies actually foretell everything that happened in

Tibet, including the corruption. For example, the prophecies tell us that in the end Tibet would be conquered by China, that the Chinese would enter the country in the Year of the Horse, and that they would rush in in the manner of a horse. The Chinese Communists did invade in the Year of the Horse, and they built roads from China to Tibet and all over Tibet and introduced motor vehicles. The prophecies also say something to the effect that in the Year of the Pig, the country would be reduced to the level of a pig, which refers to primitive beliefs, the indoctrination of the Tibetans with foreign ideas.

Another prophecy of Padmasambhava says that the end of Tibet would occur when the household objects of Tsang, the upper province, would be found in Kongpo, the lower province. In fact, it happened that there was a huge flood in the upper province of Tsang when the top of a glaciated mountain fell into the lake below. The whole of the Brahmaputra River was flooded, and it swept villages and monasteries along in its course. Many of the household articles from these places were found in Kongpo, where the river had carried them. His prophecies also say that another sign of the end of Tibet would be the building of a yellow temple at the foot of the Potala Palace, in Lhasa. In fact, the thirteenth Dalai Lama had a vision that a temple of Kalachakra should be built there, and they painted it yellow. Another of Padmasambhava's prophecies says that at the fourteenth stage, the rainbow of the Potala would disappear. The "fourteenth stage" refers to the time of the present, the fourteenth, Dalai Lama. Of course, the Potala is the winter palace of the Dalai Lama.

When Padmasambhava told these stories, the Tibetan king and his ministers were extremely upset, and they asked Padmasambhava to help them. "What is the best thing we can do to preserve our nation?" they asked him. "There is nothing we can do," he replied, "other than preserve the teachings that are being given now and place them in safe-keeping somewhere." Then he introduced the idea of bury-ing treasures, sacred writings.

He had various writings of his put in gold and silver con-tainers like capsules and buried in certain appropriate places in the different parts of Tibet so that people of the future would rediscover them. He also had domestic articles buried: jewelry of his, jewelry belonging to the king and the royal household, and articles from ordinary farming households as well. The idea was that people would become more primi-tive, human intelligence would regress, and people would no longer be able to work properly with their hands and pro-duce objects on that kind of artistic level.

So these things were buried all over Tibet, making use of scientific knowledge—quite possibly from India—on how best to preserve the parchments and other kinds of objects. The treasures were buried in many protective layers, includ-ing layers of charcoal, ground chalk, and other materials with various chemical properties. Also, for security, there was a layer of poison around the outside, so that thieves or other people without the right knowledge would be unable to dig them out. Such treasures have been discovered lately by great teachers who were supposedly tülkus of Padmasam-bhava's disciples. They had psychic visions (whatever those are) of certain places where they should dig. Then they set up the unburying process as a ceremony. The devotees would be assembled as well as workmen to do the digging. Some-times the treasure would have to be dug out of a rock.

This process of rediscovering the treasures has been hap-pening all along, and a lot of sacred teachings have been re-vealed. One example is *The Tibetan Book of the Dead*.

Another approach to preserving treasures of wisdom is the style of the thought lineage. Teachings have been rediscovered by certain appropriate teachers who have had memories of them and written them down from memory. This is another kind of hidden treasure.

An example of Padmasambhava's acting as a father figure for Tibet was the warning that he gave King Trisong Detsen. The New Year's celebration was about to be held, which traditionally included horse racing and archery, among the other events. Padmasambhava said, "There shouldn't be horse racing or archery this time." But the people around the king found a way to get around Padmasambhava's warning, and the king was killed by the arrow of an unknown assassin at the time of the horse racing and archery.

Padmasambhava loved Tibet and its people dearly, and one might have expected him to stay there. But another interesting part of the story is that at a certain point, he left. It seems that there is just a certain time to care for and look after situations. Once the country had gotten itself together spiritually and domestically and people had developed *some* sense of sanity, Padmasambhava left Tibet.

Padmasambhava still lives, literally. He is not living in South America, but in some remote place—on a continent of vampires, at a place there called *Sangdok Pelri,* "Glorious Copper-Colored Mountain." He still lives. Since he *is* the state of dharmakaya, the fact of physical bodies dissolving back into nature is not regarded as a big deal. So if we search for him, we might find him. But I'm sure you will be very disappointed when you see him.

Of course, we are no longer talking about his eight aspects alone. I am sure that since then he has developed millions of aspects.

STUDENT: You talked about the thought-lineage transmission. You said that the teacher creates half of it and the student creates the other half. I thought that crazy wisdom was uncreated.

TRUNGPA RINPOCHE: Yes. It is uncreated, but it is spontaneously existing. You have one half and the teacher has the other half. It wasn't manufactured on the spot; it was *there*.

STUDENT: Do you think America is savage enough for crazy wisdom?

TRUNGPA RINPOCHE: Needless to say.

STUDENT: I didn't understand a phrase you used: "living for death." Could you explain that?

TRUNGPA RINPOCHE: The usual approach to living is the notion that each time we breathe in and out we are approaching closer to death. Every hour brings us closer to death. Whereas in the case of the crazy-wisdom principle, energy is rejuvenated continuously.

STUDENT: Rinpoche, you made the statement that Guru Rinpoche is literally alive in some country. Are you serious? You used the word *literally*.

TRUNGPA RINPOCHE: At this point it is uncertain what is serious; or what is literal, for that matter.

S: So you could say anything?

TR: I suppose so.

STUDENT: You mentioned the "black air" that the teacher creates. Is part of that created by the student as well?

TRUNGPA RINPOCHE: Yes, by the student's timidity.

S: You also said if the student had doubts, the crazy-wisdom guru would take advantage of the doubts.

TR: Yes.

S: In what way might he take advantage of the student's doubts?

TR: I wonder if I should give away the game. . . . The doubt is a moment of uncertainty. For example, if you're physically weak, you can catch flu and colds easily. If you're not prepared and you're not defending yourself, you can be caught in that weak moment. That seems to be it.

STUDENT: I remember you once said that when the abhisheka was about to happen, there was a sort of moment of fear. How does that relate to insecurity and the student losing his ground?

TRUNGPA RINPOCHE: Well, any relationship between the student and the crazy-wisdom guru is regarded as an abhisheka.

STUDENT: In the case of self-existing crazy wisdom, is Padmasambhava the activator principle?

TRUNGPA RINPOCHE: The activator as well as the background. Because he also consists of dharmakaya as well as sambhogakaya and nirmanakaya.

STUDENT: You talked of the crazy-wisdom process as being one of building up and building up ego until there's a tremendous drop. But at one point you also talked about a process of hopelessness that does not come all at once but develops situationally little by little. I don't see how those two processes can go on simultaneously. They're going in opposite directions.

TRUNGPA RINPOCHE: Building you up until you have a big fall is the strategy of the crazy-wisdom teacher. Meanwhile, you go along gradually developing hopelessness.

S: When the thought-lineage transmission occurs, there's this openness, this gap. Is that in itself the transmission?

TR: Yes, that's it. Yes, that's it. And there is also the environment around that, which is somewhat global, almost creating a landscape. In the midst of that, the gap is the highlight.

S: It seems that we constantly find ourselves in situations of openness and slip out. What is the benefit of going back to it? Is it kind of a practice, seeing that space so you can go back to it?

TR: Well, you see, you can't recreate that. But you can create your own abhisheka every moment. After the first experience. After that you can develop your own inner guru; and you create your own abhisheka, rather than trying to memorize what happened already in that past. If you keep going back to that moment in the past, it becomes kind of a special treasure, which doesn't help.

S: Doesn't help?

TR: Doesn't help.

S: But it's necessary to have that experience—

TR: That experience is a catalyst. For example, if you have once had an accident, each time after that when you drive with some crazy driver, you have a really living idea of an accident. You have the sense that you might die at any moment, which is true.

STUDENT: We are talking of openness as a very special situation taking place in transmission, and yet, it seems that it's spontaneously there, subliminally and very often here and there and everywhere. It's naturally behind neurosis as it passes through you, kind of passing with it. Can you speak more about the situation of the naturalness of the openness?

TRUNGPA RINPOCHE: It seems that at this point if we try to be more specific in describing the details, it won't particularly help. It would be like creating special tactics and telling you how to reproduce them—like trying to be spontaneous by textbook—which doesn't seem to do any good. Probably we have to go through some kind of a trial period.

Notes

SEMINAR I

CHAPTER 5

1. Pön (often written "Bon") is an indigenous pre-Buddhist religion of Tibet. [Ed.]

SEMINAR II

CHAPTER 1

2. "Simultaneous birth" is a reference to the tantric notion of coemergence, or coemergent wisdom (Tib. lhenchik kyepe yeshe). Samsara and nirvana arise together, naturally giving birth to wisdom. [Ed.]

CHAPTER 2

3. This does not contradict Trungpa Rinpoche's description in the main body of this talk, of the dharmakaya as unconditioned. Although conditioned by a sense of pregnancy, the dharmakaya, as he tells us earlier, also remains unaffected by any contents, thus providing the continual possibility of a glimpse of unconditioned mind. Cf. Rinpoche's answer to the question about karma and the dharmakaya, on pages 123–124. [Ed.]

CHAPTER 3

4. Herbert V. Guenther, transl., *The Life and Teaching of Naropa* (Oxford: Oxford University Press, 1963).

CHAPTER 4

5. Francesca Fremantle and Chögyam Trungpa, transl., *The Tibetan Book of the Dead: The Great Liberation through Hearing in the Bardo* (Boston and London: Shambhala, 1987).

CHAPTER 6

6. This is a quotation from the author's *Sadhana of Mahamudra*, a liturgy practiced by his students. [Ed.]

About the Author

VEN. CHÖGYAM TRUNGPA was born in the province of Kham in Eastern Tibet in 1940. When he was just thirteen months old, Chögyam Trungpa was recognized as a major *tülku*, or incarnate teacher. According to Tibetan tradition, an enlightened teacher is capable, based on his or her vow of compassion, of reincarnating in human form over a succession of generations. Before dying, such a teacher leaves a letter or other clues to the whereabouts of the next incarnation. Later, students and other realized teachers look through these clues and, based on careful examination of dreams and visions, conduct searches to discover and recognize the successor. Thus, particular lines of teaching are formed, in some cases extending over several centuries. Chögyam Trungpa was the eleventh in the teaching lineage known as the Trungpa tülkus.

Once young tülkus are recognized, they enter a period of intensive training in the theory and practice of the Buddhist teachings. Trungpa Rinpoche (*Rinpoche* is an honorific title meaning "precious one"), after being enthroned as supreme abbot of Surmang Monasteries and governor of Surmang District, began a period of training that would last eighteen years, until his departure from Tibet in 1959. As Kagyü tülku, his training was based on the systematic practice of meditation and on refined theoretical understanding of Buddhist philosophy. One of the four great lineages of Tibet, the Kagyü is known as the "practice lineage."

At the age of eight, Trungpa Rinpoche received ordination as a novice monk. After his ordination, he engaged in intensive study and practice of the traditional monastic disciplines as well as in the arts of calligraphy, thangka painting, and monastic dance. His primary teachers were Jamgön Kongtrül of Sechen and Khenpo Kangshar—leading teachers in the Nyingma and Kagyü lineages. In 1958, at the age of eighteen, Trungpa Rinpoche completed his studies, receiving the degree of *kyorpon* (doctor of divinity) and *khenpo* (master of studies). He also received full monastic ordination.

The late fifties were a time of great upheaval in Tibet. As it became clear that the Chinese Communists intended to take over the country by force, many people, both monastic and lay, fled the country. Trungpa Rinpoche spent many harrowing months trekking over the Himalayas (described in his book *Born in Tibet*). After narrowly escaping capture by the Chinese, he at last reached India in 1959. While in India, Trungpa Rinpoche was appointed by His Holiness Tenzin Gyatso, the fourteenth Dalai Lama, to serve as spiritual advisor to the Young Lamas Home School in Dalhousie, India. He served in this capacity from 1959 to 1963.

Trungpa Rinpoche's first opportunity to encounter the West came when he received a Spaulding sponsorship to attend Oxford University. At Oxford he studied comparative religion, philosophy, and fine arts. He also studied Japanese flower arranging, receiving a degree from the Sogetsu School. While in England, Trungpa Rinpoche began to instruct Western students in the *dharma* (the teachings of the

Buddha), and in 1968 he founded the Samye Ling Meditation Centre in Dumfriesshire, Scotland. During this period he also published his first two books, both in English: *Born in Tibet* and *Meditation in Action.*

In 1969, Trungpa Rinpoche traveled to Bhutan, where he entered into a solitary meditation retreat. This retreat marked a pivotol change in his approach to teaching. Immediately upon returning he became a lay person, putting aside his monastic robes and dressing in ordinary Western attire. He also married a young Englishwoman, and together they left Scotland and moved to North America. Many of his early students found these changes shocking and upsetting. However, he expressed a conviction that, in order to take root in the West, the dharma needed to be taught free from cultural trappings and religious fascination.

During the seventies America was in a period of political and cultural ferment. It was a time of fascination with the East. Trungpa Rinpoche criticized the materialistic and commercialized approach to spirituality he encountered, describing it as a "spiritual supermarket." In his lectures, and in his books *Cutting Through Spiritual Materialism* and *The Myth of Freedom*, he pointed to the simplicity and directness of sitting meditation as the way to cut through such distortions of the spiritual journey.

During his seventeen years of teaching in North America, Trungpa Rinpoche developed a reputation as a dynamic and controversial teacher.

Fluent in the English language, he was one of the first *lamas* who could speak to Western students directly, without the aid of a translator. Traveling extensively throughout North America and Europe, Trungpa Rinpoche gave hundreds of talks and seminars. He established major centers in Vermont, Colorado, and Nova Scotia, as well as many

188 • ABOUT THE AUTHOR

smaller meditation and study centers in cities throughout North America and Europe. Vajradhatu was formed in 1973 as the central administrative body of this network.

In 1974, Trungpa Rinpoche founded the Naropa Institute, which became the only accredited Buddhist-inspired university in North America. He lectured extensively at the Institute, and his book *Journey Without Goal* is based on a course he taught there. In 1976, he established the Shambhala Training program, a series of weekend programs and seminars that provides instruction in meditation practice within a secular setting. His book *Shambhala: The Sacred Path of the Warrior* gives an overview of the Shambhala teachings.

Trungpa Rinpoche was also active in the field of translation. Working with Francesca Fremantle, he rendered a new translation of *The Tibetan Book of the Dead*, which was published in 1975. Later he formed the Nalanda Translation Committee, in order to translate texts and liturgies for his own students as well as to make important texts available publicly.

Trungpa Rinpoche was also known for his interest in the arts, and particularly for his insights into the relationship between contemplative discipline and the artistic process. His own art work included calligraphy, painting, flower arranging, poetry, playwriting, and environmental installations. In addition, at the Naropa Institute, he created an educational atmosphere that attracted many leading artists and poets. The exploration of the creative process in light of contemplative training continues there as a provocative dialogue. Trungpa Rinpoche also published two books of poetry: *Mudra* and *First Thought Best Thought*.

Trungpa Rinpoche's published books represent only a fraction of the rich legacy of his teachings. During his seventeen years of teaching in North America, he crafted the structures necessary to provide his students with thorough, systematic training in the dharma. From introductory talks and courses to advanced group retreat practices, these programs emphasize a balance of study and practice, of intellect and intuition. Students at all levels can pursue their interest in meditation and the Buddhist path through these many forms of training. Senior students of Trungpa Rinpoche continue to be involved in both teaching and meditation instruction in such programs. In addition to his extensive teachings in the Buddhist tradition, Trungpa Rinpoche also placed great emphasis on the Shambhala teachings, which stress the importance of mind-training, as distinct from religious practice; community involvement and the creation of an enlightened society; and appreciation of one's day-to-day life.

Trungpa Rinpoche passed away in 1987, at the age of forty-seven. He is survived by his wife, Diana, and five sons. By the time of his death, Trungpa Rinpoche had become known as a pivotal figure in introducing dharma to the Western world. The joining of his great appreciation for Western culture and his deep understanding of his own tradition led to a revolutionary approach to teaching the dharma, in which the most ancient and profound teachings were presented in a thoroughly contemporary way. Trungpa Rinpoche was known for his fearless proclamation of the dharma: free from hesitation, true to the purity of the tradition, and utterly fresh. May the teachings take root and flourish for the benefit of all sentient beings.

Senge Dradrok

Index

Meditation Center Information and Resources

For information about meditation instruction or to find a practice center near you, please contact one of the following:

Shambhala International
1084 Tower Road
Halifax, Nova Scotia
Canada B3H 2Y5
phone: (902) 425-4275
fax: (902) 423-2750
website: *www.shambhala.org*

Shambhala Europe
Kartäuserwall 20
D50678 Köln, Germany
phone: 49-221-31024-00
fax: 49-221-31024-50
e-mail: office@shambhala-europe.org

Karmê Chöling
369 Patneaude Lane
Barnet, Vermont 05821
phone: (802) 633-2384
fax: (802) 633-3012
e-mail: reception@karmecholing.org

Shambhala Mountain Center
151 Shambhala Way
Red Feather Lakes, Colorado 80545
phone: (970) 881-2184
fax: (970) 881-2909
e-mail: info@shambhalamountain.org

Dorje Denma Ling
2280 Balmoral Road
Tatamagouche, Nova Scotia
Canada B0K 1V0
phone: (902) 657-9085
e-mail: info@dorjedenmaling.com

Gampo Abbey
Pleasant Bay, Nova Scotia
Canada B0E 2P0
phone: (902) 224-2752
e-mail: office@gampoabbey.org

Naropa University is the only accredited, Buddhist-inspired university in North America. For more information, contact:

Naropa University
2130 Arapahoe Avenue
Boulder, Colorado 80302
phone: (303) 444-0202
e-mail: info@naropa.edu
website: *www.naropa.edu*

Audio recordings of talks and seminars by Chögyam Trungpa are available from:

Kalapa Recordings
1084 Tower Road
Halifax, Nova Scotia
Canada B3H 2Y5
phone: (902) 420-1118, ext. 121
fax: (902) 423-2750
e-mail: recordings@shambhala.org
website: *www.shambhalamedia.org*

The Chögyam Trungpa website
www.ChogyamTrungpa.com

This website includes a biography, information on new releases by and about Chögyam Trungpa, a description and order information for all of his books, plus links to related organizations.

The Ocean of Dharma E-Newsletter

Sign up for the Ocean of Dharma e-newsletter and receive a quote from Chögyam Trungpa Rinpoche every week. You'll also have access to a growing archive containing hundreds of other quotes taken from Trungpa Rinpoche's works. Go to *www.OceanofDharma.com*.